ISBN	eBook	979-8-89165-319-1
	Paperback	979-8-89165-318-4
	Hardback	979-8-218-81960-6

Cover Design by Anton Khodakovskiy
Interior Layout and Design by Anton Khodakovskiy
Editorial Team: Ginny Glass, Marcie Taylor, Kiska Carr

Published by
STREAMLINE
Kansas City, MO
shareyourstory.com

Streamline
BOOKS

FROM

CRISIS

to

CLARITY

A PROVEN FRAMEWORK TO TRANSFORM YOUR BUSINESS ON THE BRINK

ROD NEUENSCHWANDER

CONTENTS

To the two people who have had the most impact on my life. Together, they have made me a better person.

To my wife, Liz:

I am blessed beyond what I deserve to have you as my wife of twenty-five years. Our journey hasn't been easy, but it has been rich and full. Your generous and caring spirit has made me more generous and caring. Brendon, Iain, and Kaysie—our three amazing kids—are blessed to have you as their mom. I'm excited for what God has in store for us next. I love you more every day.

To John Ruhlin, my closest friend and business partner:

It has been the honor of my life to be your friend and partner for eighteen years. You had the crazy ideas; I was the consistent and boring one. But somehow, over the years, your crazy became more strategic, and my boring became bolder. I miss you every day and strive to honor your legacy. Promise kept. The book is done. Love you, brother—forever.

PROLOGUE

It was around ten thirty on a Monday morning when everything changed. I was on my morning run—a discipline I haven't missed in over fifteen years—when my neighbor suddenly pulled up alongside me. My wife had sent her to find me.

"You need to get home right now," she said, her face grave. "It's about John."

The news hit like a physical blow: John Ruhlin, my closest friend and business partner of eighteen years, had passed away unexpectedly. In an instant, my world tilted on its axis.

As I returned home, my thoughts were already swirling—not just with grief for my friend, but with the weight of responsibility that now fell squarely on my shoulders. Our team. John's family. The future of Gift·ology, the company we'd built from nothing. Every aspect of our business had been touched by John's unique abilities to connect with people and build relationships.

Within forty-eight hours of that devastating call, I faced decisions that would determine not just Gift·ology's survival but its future transformation. The company had lost its most public face, its primary lead generator, and nearly 70 percent of its most profitable revenue streams.

In those critical first days, I discovered that twenty years of helping other companies through crises had prepared me for this moment. As painful as it was, I knew what needed to be done. I sat down and did for my own company what I had done ten times for others: I built a framework for a recovery plan.

What happened next revealed everything I've learned about turning crisis into opportunity. The choices made in those first hours and days would set the trajectory for everything that followed. I could allow the crisis to dictate Gift·ology's future, or I could transform it into an opportunity to carry forward John's legacy in a new way.

That's the power of maintaining clarity while facing brutal facts. It determines not just survival, but transformation.

DON'T FEAR THE MESS

Let me leave you with this: Leading from crisis to clarity is rarely a straight path. It's messy.

I was once given a challenge, and now I pass that challenge on to you: Don't fear the mess.

There's a lot packed into those four words. A friend once told me they hold both a promise and a command.

The promise: There *will* be a mess.

The command: Don't fear it.

I hope this book offers the guidance and encouragement you need to meet that challenge head-on.

INTRODUCTION

"YOU SHOULD WRITE ABOUT HOW YOU TURN COMPANIES AROUND."
John urged me to share these stories for years. While I
was always hesitant—partly because I wasn't convinced I had
anything unique to say—his belief never wavered. He saw value
in the experiences I'd accumulated through decades of helping
companies navigate crisis and transformation.

As Gift·ology navigates its own transformation following
John's passing, the timing is perfect to honor that wish while
demonstrating these principles in real time. I suck at gifting, but
I built the system that allows people to gift like John. Now I'm
applying the same methodical approach to recovery and transformation that has worked ten times before.

I don't know if I was lucky or good through all those turnarounds, but I'm certainly ready to share what I learned along
the way. I believe I was able to, in a way, create my own luck by
shifting odds in my favor through proven principles that have
consistently worked. This book exists to share those principles
with you.

From Crisis to Clarity is for leaders facing a crisis right
now—whether it's a major event like losing a key team member
("the fire"), slow erosion of performance that's finally reached a
breaking point ("the slow leak"), leadership challenges within
your organization ("the broken mirror"), or simply chronic
underperformance where "fine" just isn't good enough anymore
(the "hamster wheel"). The principles remain the same regardless of which crisis has brought your business to the brink.

HOW TO USE THIS BOOK

In this book, you'll learn about the **One Page Recovery Plan** we used for Gift·ology, and I'll even share it with you in appendix A. You'll come away empowered to create a One Page Recovery Plan of your own as a way to bring your business back from the brink—and then some.

Just what is that One Page Recovery Plan, exactly? It's a way to cut through the chaos, a guiding light in the storm, a "back to basics" way of grounding yourself as a leader and your company, a path to simplifying your organization and your next steps by focusing on macro issues. It helps you assess where you're at with brutal honesty and helps prepare you for where you need to go in order to move forward. I thought about titling this book *Don't Fear the Mess* at first for a reason—because it might look and feel a lot like a mess when your business faces a crisis. (And look, I've been there. Throughout this book, you'll find Messy Moments—crisis stories from my own life and experiences—to remind you that you're not alone.)

When you're in the thick of it, the One Page Recovery Plan gives you a tool you can use to take the sting out and persevere through the fear. And guess what? You just might find that buried underneath that mess is a whole lot of opportunity for transformation.

While specific content varies based on organizational context, effective One Page Recovery Plans consistently include the following—all of which you'll learn to create for yourself in this book:

- **A clear purpose statement** that connects recovery activities with organizational identity
- **3–5 strategic priorities** from your Go-Forward Operating Plan

- **2–4 financial priorities** from your Go-Forward Financial Plan
- **2-4 team priorities** from your Go-Forward Team Plan

These elements create the essential foundation for effective execution during crisis. By concentrating your attention on these critical factors rather than attempting to cover everything, you can see the light at the end of the tunnel.

If you're currently in crisis mode, I recommend starting with chapter 1, following the framework, and working your way through the book methodically. The appendixes contain practical tools you can implement immediately. All told, chapters 4–6 form the foundation for your One Page Recovery Plan if your need is immediate. Chapter 7 through the conclusion include insights for the long-term health and transformation of your organization. Along the way, you'll also see sections titled "Marching Orders" (that offer actionable next steps) and "Notes from the War Room" (that provide perspective and motivation you'll need as you face your own messes). Choose your own adventure through this book, but choose wisely. Wherever you're starting from or wherever you're headed through your transformation, you can find continued support at *businessonthebrink.com*.

The truth is that every organization will face a crisis. It's not a matter of if, but when. The difference between organizations that merely survive and those that transform lies in how their leaders respond when that moment arrives or how prepared they are in advance.

Let's get started.

CHAPTER 1

EVERY ORGANIZATION WILL FACE CRISIS

IN THOSE FIRST DAYS AFTER MY BUSINESS PARTNER AND BEST FRIEND died unexpectedly, team members looked to me for answers. I'll be the first to admit that, at that point, I didn't have them all. I remember telling them honestly, "I know you're expecting me to have a plan. I'm just not there yet." But I knew I needed to find my way to clarity—quickly.

And I did. Because that's what John would have expected me to do.

By Wednesday night, seventy-two hours after receiving the news, I had developed a framework for Gift·ology's future. This wasn't just about survival; it was about honoring the mission John and I had built together. The plan emerged from a place of brutal realism about our circumstances, combined with the recognition of assets we already had but hadn't fully leveraged.

Mike Monroe, our partner who had captured John's voice and vision for years, flew in that weekend. Together, we solidified what would become Mission 600—our road map to replace the revenue streams we'd lost by accelerating educational platforms we had already begun developing. If we could secure six hundred memberships in our new community, we could not only survive but potentially exceed what we had built before.

The path forward wasn't obvious at first, but once the plan crystallized, it provided the framework we needed. It gave me the ability to communicate with clarity to our team, our partners, and our broader network. Most importantly, it gave us all something to focus on beyond our grief.

What happened next revealed everything I've learned about turning crisis into opportunity—lessons that began long before this moment, in ten business turnarounds and transformations over two decades. This experience wasn't unique; it was simply the most personal application of principles I'd been developing my entire career.

THE UNIVERSAL NATURE OF BUSINESS CRISIS

Every organization will face a crisis. This isn't pessimism—it's reality. Over twenty years working with companies across multiple industries, I've witnessed the same pattern repeatedly: Crisis doesn't discriminate based on industry, size, or leadership quality. The question isn't if your organization will face a crisis, but when—and more importantly, how will you respond when it arrives?

The forces that create business crises are built into the very nature of markets, leadership, and human psychology. Markets evolve, disrupting established business models. Leaders make decisions with imperfect information. Teams develop blind spots. Competitors emerge from unexpected places. Economic cycles turn. The world changes in ways no one predicted.

Even the most successful organizations contain the seeds of potential crisis. In fact, success itself can create vulnerability by fostering complacency or encouraging risk-taking. We've all seen companies that dominated their industries suddenly find themselves fighting for survival when the ground shifts beneath them. I've heard it said that every company is three decisions away from failure, and I believe this to be true.

This reality isn't something to fear—it's something to prepare for. Understanding the universal nature of crisis is the first step toward developing the mindset and tools needed to navigate it successfully.

MESSY MOMENT: YOUR CURRENT SITUATION DOES NOT MAKE YOU A BAD PERSON

Sadly, I have seen founders view themselves as lacking integrity while experiencing a tough time. Outsiders don't always help. I was once asked to attend a conservative Mennonite church meeting to defend a struggling founder. There was a clear assumption from those in attendance that this member lacked integrity because he could not pay his bills.

I remember thinking during the meeting, *This isn't helping, and if you are not going to write a check, then keep your mouth shut.* Making a miscalculation (or whatever caused your current situation) does not make you a bad person. What you do next, though, might.

I have witnessed founders try shortcuts. To bridge a cash gap, a founder once "sold" products to a family member for customer financing, and then didn't pay off the floor plan lender because "money was promised" from a friend. Guess what? The "money" never came. That is an integrity issue.

Do your best to block out the noise and focus on executing the recovery plan you establish using this book. I commonly tell founders to ignore comments from those not in the room. I promise you they will praise your grit later.

> Dwight Mason, an early mentor of mine, once told me, "People are like tea. You don't know what's inside until you put them in hot water." Perhaps your current situation is an opportunity to show who you really are.

Through my work with ten organizations, I've found that crises typically fall into four categories:

- **The Fire (or Dramatic Event Crisis):** The most dramatic crisis—sudden, unexpected changes that demand immediate response. These might include the loss of a key leader (as with John's passing), the abrupt exit of a major client representing a significant portion of revenue, regulatory changes that undermine your business model, or external events like economic downturns or global disruptions. These crises announce themselves loudly and force immediate decisions.

- **The Slow Leak (or Unaddressed Erosion):** This is what I call "acceptable decline"—problems you know exist but don't address because they haven't yet become urgent. Perhaps your margins are gradually shrinking, your customer satisfaction scores are trending downward, or your once-innovative product is becoming commoditized. These situations don't trigger alarm bells, but they steadily weaken your foundation until a breaking point arrives.

- **The Broken Mirror (or Leadership Challenges):** These occur when the leaders themselves become obstacles to the organization's health. This might involve founders whose skills no longer match the company's growth stage, executives whose personal issues affect their performance, or leadership teams divided by conflict. These situations are particularly challenging because those who might initiate change are often part of the problem.

- **The Hamster Wheel (or Chronic Underperformance):** This happens when "fine" isn't good enough. Your organization isn't failing, but it's consistently falling short of its potential. You're profitable but not growing. You're stable but not innovating. You're surviving but not thriving. This type of crisis rarely feels urgent, which is precisely what makes it dangerous—it can persist for years, slowly diminishing your organization's vitality and relevance.

I've seen organizations overcome devastating setbacks and emerge stronger. I've also watched companies with minor challenges spiral into decline because they couldn't or wouldn't respond effectively. The distinguishing factor isn't the magnitude of the crisis—it's the quality of the response. Organizations that survive and ultimately thrive through crisis share common characteristics: They face reality honestly, they maintain calm amid chaos, they simplify their organization through macro thinking, and they align their team around clear priorities.

These capabilities aren't innate—they're developed through intentional practice. The methodologies I've refined through ten turnarounds provide a framework for developing these capabilities before crisis strikes, so when it inevitably arrives, you're prepared to respond effectively.

MY CRISIS EDUCATION: LEARNING IN THE TRENCHES

My education in crisis management didn't come from business school—it came from the trenches. Long before I developed frameworks or systems, I was thrown into situations that demanded immediate action with limited information. These experiences shaped my approach to crisis response more profoundly than any textbook could. You should also know that I'm not trained in finance. Instead, I *learned* it, mainly by studying a few grad-level courses in accounting and finance and by getting a real-world education of those principles in action. My actual undergrad degree is in psychology with a minor in political science, and I am living proof that you don't have to be expertly trained to understand finances. That is not a valid excuse for not understanding the basics.

My career in turnarounds began unexpectedly. After college, while working for a consulting firm, I met John Ruhlin at a Christian concert. Though we'd both attended Malone University, we hadn't known each other there. We hit it off immediately during a two-hour lunch that ended with us declaring we needed to buy companies together.

Our first target was a retail furniture business in Ohio's Amish country—a company where both of us knew the owner. We never anticipated it would become my first turnaround experience. I was hired as president at just twenty-five years old, walking into what I thought was a stable but declining business, only to discover they'd just completed their first year without making money.

I had no playbook. No experience. No real understanding of what I was facing. But I had to make decisions—real decisions with real consequences for real people. This baptism by fire taught me the necessity of staying calm under pressure and the importance of focusing on fundamental business drivers rather than getting lost in details. As you can imagine, I didn't display these traits right out of the gate, but I quickly noted their necessity in crisis and made it a point to learn.

While we ultimately didn't purchase that company, the experience gave me something far more valuable—the beginning of a methodology for understanding and addressing business crises.

Shortly after that first experience, John connected me with an opportunity in Eastern Pennsylvania that would test everything I thought I knew about business. My wife and I moved across state lines to take on not one struggling company, but five different operating companies under common ownership—retail furniture, trucking, RV dealerships, and more.

The situation was dire. A major accounting error had masked significant losses in the retail furniture operation. To cover those losses, they'd borrowed against their trucking fleet, putting a large amount of debt on aging equipment. The RV dealerships operated under a strange partnership where we managed sales but didn't own the inventory.

This complex, interconnected mess demanded immediate action. Over the next two years, I found myself shutting down an underperforming location just before Christmas. I negotiated with floor plan lenders to voluntarily surrender inventory we couldn't afford. I found myself on the phone with a bank, saying, "Either you accept this deal right now, or you can come pick up your collateral—but I need funds wired today to make payroll."

The pressure was relentless, the decisions painful, and the learning curve vertical. But from this chaotic period emerged principles that would guide every turnaround I led afterward: Simplify your organization by focusing on macro issues.

When we eventually stabilized and sold the furniture retailer, I drove back to Ohio with a cigar, thinking, *I can't believe we pulled that off.* I didn't know then that these experiences were preparing me for even greater challenges ahead—including the transformation of a struggling promotional products business into what would become Gift·ology.

LESSONS LEARNED FROM A ONE-ARMED DAIRY FARMER

The foundation for my approach to crisis was laid long before my business career began—on a dairy farm in Amish country, Ohio. When I was three years old, my father lost his right arm in a farm accident. For a right-handed dairy farmer, this should have been career-ending. But when people asked him what he was going to do now, his answer was simple: "I'm going to farm."

And farm he did—for over fifty years, without hired help beyond his four children. He had to relearn everything, becoming left-hand dominant. He adapted tools, changed techniques, and found new ways to accomplish familiar tasks. What strikes me most in retrospect is that I never once heard him complain. Not a single time.

My father faced the brutal facts of his reality and moved forward anyway. He didn't deny the severity of his situation, but he refused to be defined or limited by it. He understood that circumstances don't determine outcomes—responses do.

From my father, I learned that acceptance of reality is not the same as surrender to it. Adaptation isn't just about survival— it's about finding new ways to thrive. Resilience comes from daily decisions, not grand gestures. Forward movement, even when difficult, is always better than frozen indecision.

These lessons would prove invaluable when John and I merged forces to transform a struggling business into what would become Gift·ology—a journey that began, like so many successful ventures, in the midst of crisis.

THE BIRTH OF GIFTO·LOGY THROUGH CRISIS

When John and I finally joined forces, he was candid about his situation: "I think the wheels are falling off." Despite being Cutco's number one salesperson and having an extraordinary gift for building relationships, his business was losing money. The company—then called Ruhlin Promotion Group—was in trouble.

John was brilliant at networking and relationship building—truly world-class—but running an operation requires different skills. He had made investments in companies that weren't performing well. He had purchased a property in southern Ohio that was draining cash. He had overinvested in real estate where he wanted to live. Money was flowing out faster than it was coming in.

His superpower—connecting authentically with people—wasn't translating into business success because the operational infrastructure wasn't there to support it. His calendar was chaotic, his focus scattered across too many opportunities, and his team unsure of priorities. Without structure, even John's remarkable talent couldn't prevent financial decline.

For the first year after combining forces, we each took only $1,500 per month—and my wife and I didn't even cash those checks, as we knew there wasn't enough money to cover them. We were starting essentially from zero, with debt to manage and a business model that wasn't working.

Financial pressure forced us to rethink everything. We couldn't continue trying to serve every industry in every geography—we didn't have the resources. We had to identify where our limited energy and capital would generate the greatest return.

We observed that our most successful client relationships shared something in common: They weren't defined by industry but by mindset. They were generous people who understood the power of relationships in their world. This realization led to a pivotal shift—what if, instead of trying to reach everyone, we focused on reaching these people specifically?

This led John to begin speaking at events where relationship-oriented leaders gathered. His first paid speaking engagement brought in $5,000—a significant sum for us at the time. We reinvested these funds to create more speaking opportunities, which generated more clients, which funded more speaking engagements. This virtuous cycle eventually transformed our business model.

What had begun as a financial necessity—focusing our limited resources on a specific audience—became our strategic advantage. The crisis had forced us to abandon a broad, unfocused approach for something more targeted and effective.

During this time, I was approached by our lawyer, who knew I had a history working with failing companies, to ask if I would be willing to help one of his clients. John and I decided I would help his client mainly because we needed the money. That decision was the origin of Ruhlin Partners. Through this less public company, John and I partnered with ten founders struggling through one of the four crises. Since then, Ruhlin Partners has helped generate over $30 million of wealth creation events for our partners, provided the funds for Gift·ology to scale, and developed the principles I am sharing with you in this book.

As our business began to grow, it became clear that John and I approached the world very differently. His genius was in relationship building and visionary thinking; mine was in operations and strategy. These complementary strengths could be powerful—but only if we aligned our efforts.

Out of this need, I developed what we called The Ruhlin Way—a set of guiding principles that would align our decision-making and operations. These ten insights included fundamentals like focusing on balance sheet strength, prioritizing gross profit over mere revenue, seeking wise counsel, and building margins of safety into every deal.

This framework wasn't theoretical—it emerged from real challenges we faced. It became our shared language for decision-making, helping us avoid conflicts and misunderstandings that might otherwise have derailed our partnership.

Most importantly, it allowed us to design our organization around John's strengths rather than trying to change him. I realized trying to make John better at operations—moving him from a three to a five on a scale of ten—would still result in failure. Instead, we built systems that allowed him to spend 80 percent of his time talking to people, which is what he did better than anyone I've ever met.

As I reflect on our journey with Gift·ology—and the turnarounds I've led over the years—I've come to recognize a pattern: Crisis creates possibilities that comfort never could. When systems are working, there's little incentive to question fundamental assumptions or explore radically different approaches. Crisis strips away that complacency.

The pivot that led to Gift·ology's success and the creation of Ruhlin Partners would never have happened without financial pressure forcing us to rethink our business model. The Ruhlin Way would never have been created without the misalignments that threatened our partnership. Our most important innovations emerged not from comfort but from necessity.

This pattern holds true across organizations and industries. The companies that emerge strongest from crisis are those that use it as an opportunity to challenge assumptions, use macro thinking to refocus on fundamentals, and reimagine possibilities.

They don't just survive crisis—they transform through it.

This understanding—that crisis contains the seeds of opportunity—doesn't make it pleasant. When you're in the middle of it, the pressure is real and the stress is significant. But recognizing this pattern can provide the confidence needed to move forward, even when the path isn't yet clear.

INITIAL RESPONSE PROTOCOL:
THE FIRST SEVENTY-TWO HOURS

The first seventy-two hours after a crisis emerges are critical. During this window, you establish patterns and trajectories that can be difficult to change later. I've found that in virtually every turnaround situation, the steps taken—or not taken—in these first three days dramatically influence outcomes.

In the immediate aftermath of a crisis, two opposing forces threaten effective response: Paralysis and panic. Paralysis comes from the overwhelming nature of the situation—there are so many problems that it's difficult to know where to begin. Panic, on the other hand, drives rushed decisions without proper consideration of their long-term implications.

Those first seventy-two hours establish not just your initial response, but the mindset your organization will carry forward. If you respond with calm, methodical clarity, that becomes your organization's approach to the challenges ahead. If you respond with scattered, reactionary decisions, that becomes your pattern as well.

I experienced this vividly after John's passing. I needed to move quickly—our team was looking for direction, and our network was eager to help. But moving quickly without clarity would have been disastrous. Taking those first three days to develop a coherent plan allowed us to harness the goodwill and energy of our network rather than dissipating it in well-meaning but uncoordinated efforts.

When you find your business on the brink, pull yourself up out of the details. This book will help guide you through this process and develop your One Page Recovery Plan for recovery.

These questions create the foundation for your initial response. They force you to confront reality while focusing your attention on factors you can control.

Communication in crisis requires extraordinary discipline. Your team is watching closely—not just listening to your words but observing your tone, demeanor, and consistency. This creates both challenges and opportunities. Here's what I've learned:

- **Acknowledge reality openly.** Your team already knows there's a problem. Pretending otherwise destroys credibility. I've found that stating brutal facts clearly builds confidence— it demonstrates you're in touch with reality.

- **Share what you know and admit what you don't.** When I met with our Gift·ology team after John's passing, I had to acknowledge that I didn't yet have all the answers. This honesty builds trust more effectively than false certainty.

- **Emphasize what remains stable.** In turbulence, people seek solid ground. Identify what isn't changing—your core values, commitment to clients, or long-term mission—to provide psychological anchors.

- **Focus on immediate priorities**. Give clear direction about what needs to happen today and this week. Keep these directives simple and specific. At the same time, avoid premature promises. Don't make commitments you can't keep about job security, financial recovery, or timelines. These create expectations that, if unmet, will destroy trust when you need it most.

- **Don't assign blame.** Crisis response requires forward focus. Regardless of how you got here, energy spent on blame is energy diverted from solutions.

- **Resist the urge to minimize.** Phrases like "this is just a bump in the road" or "we'll be fine" feel reassuring but can backfire by suggesting you don't grasp the situation's gravity.

- **Don't share untested theories.** Your team needs clarity, not speculation. Keep your evolving hypotheses within your crisis team until they're validated.

- **Pay attention to the timing.** I've found that the right communication cadence is crucial. In those first seventy-two hours, brief, daily updates maintain connection without creating information overload. As your response solidifies, you can shift to a more structured schedule aligned with your action plan.

- **Keep a clear head.** Clear thinking is your most valuable asset in crisis—and the most difficult to maintain. The pressure to act, the emotional weight of the situation, and the barrage of incoming information all conspire to cloud judgment exactly when you need it most. Creating mental space for clarity requires intentional practice. I've found that my clearest insights rarely come while staring at spreadsheets or sitting in emergency meetings. They emerge during runs, in prayer, in quiet moments before dawn, or sometimes even while doing mundane tasks that allow my mind to process in the background.

- **Develop a routine.** In crisis, routines provide stability that frees mental capacity. The consistency of my running habit has been crucial during turnarounds—not just for the activity itself, but for the predictable structure it creates.

- **Set boundaries around information flow.** Crisis generates an avalanche of data, opinions, and suggestions. Not all require your immediate attention. Create filters that protect your mental bandwidth for the most critical decisions.

- **Maintain physical resilience.** Sleep, nutrition, and movement aren't luxuries during a crisis—they're necessities for cognitive function. Even small commitments in these areas yield outsized benefits for decision quality.

- **Seek perspective through trusted advisers.** The right advisers don't just offer solutions—they help you see patterns and possibilities you might miss in the pressure of the moment. Choose wisely; not all advice is equally valuable in a crisis.

I experienced the power of this approach after John's passing. Despite the emotional toll and organizational uncertainty, taking time to find clarity before acting allowed us to develop a coherent plan rather than a collection of reactive decisions. By Wednesday night, seventy-two hours after receiving the news, Mike and I had developed what would become Mission 600—our framework for moving forward.

This clear-thinking space isn't a luxury—it's essential. The decisions you make in crisis have amplified consequences, both positive and negative. Creating conditions that support your best thinking is perhaps the most important investment you can make in those critical first days.

MARCHING ORDERS: THE ASSESSMENT FRAMEWORK

The point of the Assessment Framework is to gather data for your One Page Recovery Plan. Remember that as you move forward. The key is to focus on the macro level and simplify. You are not solving the problem—only gathering information. Outside perspective from trusted sources is key. I was able to accomplish this myself because I have learned how to step back over the years, but you will likely need a guide. My hope is that this book could be that for you.

Let's get into it: Most struggling organizations fixate on financial metrics—and with good reason. Financial distress is often the most visible and urgent symptom of crisis. But focusing exclusively on financial statements is like treating symptoms while ignoring the underlying condition.

When assessing financial health, compare your P&L performance to those best in class in your industry. Where is your organization falling short? Additionally, look beyond the P&L to things like cash flow projections, balance sheet analysis, debt structure evaluation, *your* key economic drivers, and the key economic drivers that have predictable revenue and scalable cost centers. In every turnaround I've led, understanding the true financial position was critical. At this stage, the one truth that you must understand is that companies fail because they run out of cash. Understanding your runway is critical. (We'll go into runway considerations in more detail later in chapter 5, and I've included an example runway calculator for you in appendix B).

PEOPLE, PROCESSES, AND POSITIONING

Within this assessment framework, I've found that three elements deserve particular attention: People, processes, and positioning. These represent the fundamental capabilities that determine an organization's ability to transform through crisis.

People assessment looks beyond formal roles and responsibilities to understand who demonstrates calm under pressure, who maintains focus on priorities despite distractions, who communicates effectively and transparently, who takes ownership rather than assigning blame, and who adapts quickly to changing circumstances.

Often, the formal leadership structure doesn't align with these critical capabilities. Your assessment needs to identify both the formal and informal leaders who will drive transformation. Sometimes the person with the right title isn't the right person for crisis leadership.

I experienced this repeatedly in turnaround situations. In one technology company that was hemorrhaging cash, we discovered that the founder's spouse—who had been playing a limited administrative role—possessed exceptional operational discipline. By elevating her role, we created the structure needed for the founder to focus on client relationships and technical vision—his strengths—while ensuring consistent execution throughout the organization.

Process assessment examines how work actually happens, not just how it's supposed to happen. Which processes create consistent results versus unpredictable outcomes? Where do bottlenecks and decision delays regularly occur? How does information flow (or doesn't flow) across teams? Which activities consume disproportionate resources? Where do quality issues repeatedly emerge?

Crisis often reveals process weaknesses that were hidden during growth periods. What worked at a smaller scale or with fewer complexities may break under pressure. Your assessment needs to identify which processes require immediate redesign versus those that can be refined over time.

Positioning assessment explores your relationship with your market. Which offerings generate consistent demand? Which customer segments provide sustainable profitability? What value propositions resonate most strongly? Where is competitive pressure increasing or decreasing? Which market trends create opportunity or threat?

When resources are constrained, as they inevitably are during a crisis, you can't pursue every opportunity or serve every market effectively. Your assessment must identify where to focus limited resources for maximum impact.

UNCOVERING HIDDEN ASSETS

One of the most valuable outcomes from an assessment is the identification of assets and opportunities that were previously overlooked. In nearly every turnaround I've led, we discovered strengths that weren't being fully leveraged or opportunities that had been obscured by day-to-day operations.

In one struggling e-commerce business, we realized that while the retail operation was barely sustainable, the founder had built sophisticated software to manage inventory across multiple sales platforms. This discovery led to a complete pivot, transforming the company from a retailer into a software-and-service platform that helped brand owners manage their e-commerce operations. This transition became the core business, eventually leading to significant outside investment.

With Gift·ology after John's passing, our assessment revealed that Mike Monroe—who had been creating our content for years—had developed an extraordinarily deep understanding of John's approach to relationship building. This realization led us to accelerate the development of our educational platform with Mike at the center, creating a new growth path that aligned with our strengths.

These hidden assets often exist in plain sight—they're overlooked not because they're invisible but because the organization hasn't recognized their full value. A fresh assessment during crisis creates the opportunity to see these assets with new eyes.

NOTES FROM THE WAR ROOM

If you complete your Marching Orders from above, you know an assessment is valuable but only if it leads to decisive action. I've encountered organizations that become trapped in analysis paralysis—endlessly refining their understanding while conditions continue to deteriorate. The discipline of assessment must be balanced with the discipline of execution.

The test of an effective assessment isn't its comprehensiveness—it's whether it enables better decisions and more focused action. If your assessment doesn't change what you do tomorrow and next week, it hasn't served its purpose.

This balance between assessment and action doesn't mean rushing to implement half-formed plans. It means ensuring that every element of your assessment connects directly to choices and priorities. The result should be a clear direction that allows your organization to move forward with conviction, even amid uncertainty.

CHAPTER 2

LEAD YOURSELF FIRST

THE WEEK AFTER JOHN'S PASSING HIT LIKE A HURRICANE. OUR team was devastated, clients were calling with concern, and media inquiries were flooding in. Yet somehow, I found myself prepared for this unimaginable moment. Twenty years of helping other companies through crisis had unknowingly trained me for the most personal crisis of my career.

The week we learned of John's passing, I still laced up my running shoes. As my feet hit the pavement in rhythm, the mental fog began to clear. With each mile, I separated emotion from strategy, grief from action. This wasn't about suppressing feelings; it was about creating space to process them while maintaining the clarity needed to lead.

By mile three, I had mentally outlined our communication strategy. By mile four, I'd identified the three immediate business priorities. By mile five, I'd determined which team members needed what kind of support. The running discipline that had seemed like just physical maintenance for years revealed itself as essential mental infrastructure in crisis.

When I returned home, showered, and sat at my desk, I opened my notebook with steady hands. The path forward wasn't easy, but it was clear. This is exactly how to maintain the clear mind and calm spirit essential for crisis leadership.

THE FOUNDATION OF CRISIS LEADERSHIP

Crisis leadership begins with self-leadership. When your business faces existential threat, everyone looks to you—not just for decisions but for cues on how to respond emotionally. Your state of mind becomes contagious. If you project panic, the organization will spiral. If you embody steady resolve, the team will rally.

I cannot overstate the danger of emotional decision-making during crisis. When threatened, our brains are biologically programmed for fight-or-flight, triggering impulses that served our ancestors well when escaping predators but today sabotage complex business recovery. Adrenaline narrows our focus precisely when we need expansive thinking, and fear accelerates decision-making when patience might reveal better options.

Your mindset affects everyone around you in ways you may not realize. Team members study your facial expressions, tone of voice, and body language for signals about the severity of the situation. They mirror your energy level and emotional state, multiplying either your panic or your composure throughout the organization.

This principle became crystal clear when teaching my son how to lead as captain of his soccer team.

"Bad things happen on the soccer pitch, and sometimes you are unlucky," I told him, "but your team is watching you. They will follow your lead either positively or negatively, so eyes up, back straight!"

The same is true if your business is on the brink. Your team will steer toward what captures your attention, whether obstacle or opportunity.

CLEAR MIND, CALM SPIRIT:
THE LEADER'S FIRST RESPONSIBILITY

Your first responsibility in crisis isn't to save the business—it's to maintain the clear mind and calm spirit necessary to make sound decisions. Panic never helps. It distorts perception, rushes judgment, and spreads like wildfire through an organization. When you feel it rising, recognize it as a signal not to act but to pause.

Creating space for clarity requires discipline. My running habit isn't just exercise; it's deliberate mental preparation. The rhythmic movement creates what psychologists call "transient hypofrontality"—a state where the brain's executive function temporarily steps back, allowing deeper insights to emerge. Find your equivalent—whether running, walking, swimming, or sitting in silence—and guard this practice fiercely during crisis and out of it.

Prayer and reflection provide guidance you can't find in spreadsheets. In stillness, separated from the noise of urgent demands, you can reconnect with foundational principles and values. These moments of vertical connection often reveal horizontal solutions that weren't visible in the chaos. I've never made a decision I regret after spending time in prayer, but I've made many I wish I could take back when rushing under pressure.

Learn to recognize when you're too close to the problem to see it clearly. Warning signs include circular thinking, inability to prioritize, emotional volatility, and loss of sleep. When these appear, it's time to create distance—physical, temporal, or mental—before making critical decisions. Sometimes the most productive action is to step away briefly, allowing your subconscious mind to process what your conscious mind cannot yet solve.

BE A CONSULTANT TO YOUR OWN COMPANY

Objectivity is your greatest asset in crisis, yet it's hardest to maintain when everything feels personal. Founders especially struggle to separate themselves from their companies, making clear-eyed assessment nearly impossible. The solution? Mentally step outside and view your business as a consultant would.

Imagine you've been hired to evaluate your current situation with no emotional attachment to past decisions, sunk costs, or personal identity. What would you immediately identify as the core issues? Which problems would you tackle first? What resources would you leverage that might be currently overlooked?

Seeing your situation through an outside lens often reveals both problems and solutions that weren't visible from within. When I work with companies in turnaround situations, I always ask these questions first:

- Which customers or product lines are actually profitable when all costs are considered?

- What products or services are customers happy to pay us for?

- Of those, products or services, which include predictable revenue and are supported by easily scalable cost centers?

- What activities consume resources without creating proportional value?

- What are you not facing that needs to be faced?

These questions strip away justifications and narratives, leaving only essential realities. They create emotional distance that allows for better solutions—not because emotions aren't valuable, but because they shouldn't be the primary filter for strategic decisions during crisis.

UNDERSTANDING FOUNDER PSYCHOLOGY

The psychological dynamics of founders under pressure create unique challenges during crisis. Understanding these patterns—in yourself or the founders you serve—is essential for effective intervention and support.

I once had a manager of one of the business units for a company I was hired to turn around storm into my office to express his frustration with the founder—the person who had hired me. In his anger, he spewed a combination of saliva and chewing tobacco all over my desk and declared loudly that the founder "had a propensity for self-destruction." I recall thinking, *Well, he isn't wrong.*

As it turns out, many founders have a propensity for self-destruction, especially during crisis. The same qualities that drive entrepreneurial success, like confidence, conviction, risk tolerance, and optimism, can become liabilities when reality contradicts the founder's vision. Rather than adjust course, many founders double down on failing strategies, alienate supporters, or make increasingly desperate moves to prove their original judgment correct.

Identity and company become dangerously intertwined for many entrepreneurs. Is this you? When your sense of self is embedded in your business, its challenges become existential threats rather than solvable problems. Learning to separate who you are from what you do creates the psychological space necessary for objective decision-making. This separation isn't abandonment—it's the healthy distance needed to save what matters most.

The fear of loss paralyzes many founders precisely when decisive action is most needed. Loss aversion—our tendency to prefer avoiding losses over acquiring equivalent gains—intensifies during crisis. This psychological principle explains why founders often resist cutting underperforming products or divisions even when doing so would clearly benefit the whole. Recognizing this bias allows you to counteract it consciously.

John and I balanced each other through complementary tendencies. His "fear of missed opportunity" drove constant exploration and innovation, while my focus on strategy and consistent execution provided stability and follow-through. During crisis, these differences became even more pronounced. Understanding your natural tendencies and surrounding yourself with complementary perspectives creates resilience your company wouldn't have otherwise.

Founder psychology can help or hinder during crisis. The visionary thinking that launches companies can generate creative solutions to seemingly impossible problems. The tenacity that overcomes startup challenges becomes the persistence needed for recovery. The challenge is channeling these strengths appropriately while mitigating the shadow sides that emerge under pressure.

BUILDING EFFECTIVE SUPPORT SYSTEMS

No leader navigates crisis effectively in isolation. The pressure, complexity, and emotional weight demand robust support systems deliberately constructed before they're desperately needed.

Creating your crisis cabinet begins with identifying two or three individuals who bring diverse perspectives, relevant experience, and uncompromising honesty. This inner circle isn't about friendship or comfort—it's about assembling the specific wisdom, skills, and viewpoints needed during turbulence.

The importance of brutally honest advisers is top of the list because crisis amplifies our natural tendencies toward self-deception and wishful thinking. Surround yourself with people committed to truth-telling even when it's painful. A diplomatic lie that spares your feelings today may cost jobs tomorrow. Make it explicitly clear that you're not seeking validation but genuine insight, and demonstrate that you value candor by acting on uncomfortable truths.

Finding guides who've weathered similar storms provides both practical wisdom and emotional reassurance. There's profound comfort in knowing someone else has survived what you're facing. These battle-tested mentors can distinguish between normal crisis patterns and truly exceptional challenges, helping you calibrate your response appropriately. They also serve as living proof that there's life beyond your current circumstances.

Isolation amplifies poor decision-making through several mechanisms: It removes critical feedback loops, creates echo chambers that reinforce existing biases, elevates emotional reactions over rational analysis, and increases psychological burden. Even brief periods of intentional connection with your support system can break these dangerous patterns and restore perspective.

THE FOUR CLARITY QUESTIONS

If your business is on the brink, turn to basic frameworks to provide essential structure for your thinking. In every turnaround situation I've faced, I return to four fundamental questions that cut through complexity and emotion to reveal core truths. Not surprisingly, these align with the One Page Recovery Plan elements we'll learn more about in chapter 4. For now, let's get to know them a little better:

- **"What's actually happening?"** Not what you fear might happen or what you hope is happening, but the objective reality of your current situation. This requires ruthless honesty and robust fact-gathering. What are your exact cash reserves? What specific customer behaviors have changed? Which obligations are truly time-sensitive? Document these realities without interpretation or justification.

- **"What's not changing?"** Amid crisis, we naturally fixate on what's breaking down. Equally important is recognizing stable elements—customer needs that remain consistent, team strengths that stand the test of time, competitive advantages that haven't eroded. These stable factors often provide the foundation for recovery.

- **"What conversation am I avoiding?"** This question requires courage. Crisis often reveals problems that existed long before the precipitating event—underperforming divisions, toxic team members, unsustainable customer relationships. These issues now demand attention you previously withheld. Identifying and addressing these overdue conversations transforms crisis into opportunity for overdue correction. The truth is you likely knew this needed to be addressed, but you haven't acted on it. I'm guilty of this too!

- **"What does success look like six months from now?"** Crisis response requires both immediate action and directional clarity. Without a concrete vision of success beyond survival, your team will lack motivation and may make shortsighted trade-offs. Define specific, achievable outcomes that constitute meaningful recovery, then work backward to identify critical path actions.

DISTINGUISHING SIGNAL FROM NOISE

Crisis floods leaders with information—some critical, much irrelevant. Developing the ability to distinguish signal from noise becomes essential for effective response and maintaining mental clarity.

True signals indicate fundamental shifts requiring your attention—significant revenue declines, major customer departures, regulatory actions, or competitive disruptions that threaten your core business. These deserve full focus and rapid response. Noise, on the other hand, includes temporary fluctuations, isolated incidents, or peripheral issues that don't impact essential operations.

The most dangerous noise often comes disguised as urgent signals—the angry but ultimately inconsequential customer resulting from an isolated incident, the alarming but statistically insignificant quality issue, or the competitor announcement that generates headlines without changing market dynamics. These distractions consume precious bandwidth you would have been better off devoting to core challenges.

Effective filtering begins with clear priorities. Here's what to know:

- *Before* **crisis hits, define the three to five metrics that truly matter for organizational health.** During turbulence, evaluate all incoming information against these critical indicators. Does this development impact our ability to serve core customers? Does it affect our cash position? Does it threaten key talent retention? If not, it may require monitoring but not immediate action.

- **Create information hierarchies that manage your attention.** Not all sources deserve equal weight—frontline employees often have better real-time insights than middle management; long-term customers provide more valuable feedback than new ones; financial institutions have different incentives than vendors when communicating challenges. Weight these inputs appropriately.

- **Develop deliberate practices for noise reduction.** This might include media fasts during critical decision periods, designated times for email and communication review, or delegating specific team members to filter and prioritize incoming information. These boundaries protect your mental bandwidth.

THE COURAGE TO MAKE HARD CALLS

Crisis leadership eventually demands decisions no one wants to make—laying off valued team members, closing locations with community impact, discontinuing unprofitable products and services with loyal customers, or making painful financial restructuring choices. These moments test not just your analytical capabilities but your leadership courage.

Hard calls share common characteristics: They involve clear trade-offs between competing values, they affect people you care about, they carry both immediate consequences and future implications, and they reveal your true priorities more clearly than any mission statement. Most importantly, they cannot be delegated or delayed without compounding damage.

The foundation for courage begins with clarity about your nonnegotiable values and responsibilities. As leader, your primary obligation is to ensure the survival and long-term viability of your organization. Without this, all other values—including employee retention and customer commitment—don't matter.

Timing matters here. Act too quickly, and you might create unnecessary disruption or miss emerging alternatives; wait too long, and options narrow while resources deplete. My experience suggests it's better to make hard calls slightly earlier than feels comfortable—the cost of premature action is typically less than the compound interest paid on delayed decisions.

Execution matters as much as the decision itself. How you implement difficult choices puts your values on full display more clearly than any corporate communication. Treat affected individuals with dignity, provide maximum support within your means, communicate transparently about the reasoning, and personally own the consequences rather than deflecting responsibility.

The courage to make hard calls doesn't develop in crisis—it's built through smaller decisions that progressively strengthen your resolve muscle. Practice making clear choices in lower-stakes situations and explicitly acknowledging trade-offs rather than pretending ideal solutions exist. These experiences create the foundation for moral courage when truly difficult moments arrive.

MESSY MOMENT: WHEN THE FBI CALLS ABOUT A MURDER

Prior to John and I combining forces, I was leading a challenging turnaround comprised of several operating companies. One of the companies was an RV dealership with several locations. Actually, the arrangement was the strangest partnership that I have ever witnessed. Our inventory was owned by the company that owned 50 percent of our dealerships. I don't understand why the owner of that company partnered with the founder I was helping because he carried the bulk of the capital risk. Strange as it was, though, that was the arrangement.

I was working for the founder when the devastating flooding happened in New Orleans. Not long later, FEMA needed 145,000 RV trailers to house those who lost their homes. The partner who owned the inventory was among many RV dealerships across the country that rushed to fulfill trailers.

Our team jumped in to help.

During this time, we purchased and sold over six hundred trailers. Needless to say, there was a lot of brokering going on across the country to secure trailers. Our team was buying trailers from a lot of people we didn't know. Months later, we received a call from the FBI. They were following up on a murder case involving someone we purchased trailers from during the scramble.

Apparently, the victim was the middleman but failed to pay for the trailers he sold us. We paid him and confirmed the transaction with the FBI. We watched the news for weeks but never found out what the rest of the story was.

Which is fine by me!

THE RECOVERY HORIZON: PLANNING BEYOND SURVIVAL

Crisis narrows focus to immediate survival, but effective leadership requires simultaneously maintaining longer recovery horizons. Without this dual vision, short-term actions can undermine long-term viability even as they address immediate threats.

Recovery planning begins by distinguishing between stopgap measures and sustainable solutions. Emergency cost-cutting, staffing adjustments, and operational triage are necessary but insufficient. True recovery requires rebuilding foundational strengths, often by addressing vulnerabilities that existed before crisis hit.

Don't forget to learn along the way. Document key learnings, unexpected discoveries, and successful adaptations. These insights often reveal new capabilities, more efficient approaches, or exciting market opportunities. The companies that emerge strongest often institutionalize adaptations born from necessity.

It's also important to evolve your messaging. Early crisis communication naturally emphasizes urgency, sacrifice, and immediate action. As stabilization occurs, I recommend gradually shifting toward growth language, capability building, and future opportunity. This transition signals confidence while acknowledging the reality of the situation.

The recovery horizon requires balancing three competing timeframes, each requiring different metrics, decision criteria, and resource allocation. Effective leaders explicitly manage these parallel tracks rather than moving sequentially from one to the next:

- **Immediate survival (0–30 days) and Stabilization (1–6 months)**. If you're in these stages, create your One Page Plan in chapters 4–6.

- **Renewal (6+ months).** If you're in this stage, learn how to move toward transformation in chapter 7 and the conclusion.

Maybe most importantly, recovery planning provides essential hope during dark moments. Teams can endure remarkable challenges when they believe their sacrifices contribute to meaningful renewal rather than merely postponing inevitable failure.

A compelling recovery vision creates resilience that even the *best* plan, on its own, cannot inspire in teams.

The best time to be the leader your team needs you to be is now.

LEADERSHIP COMMUNICATION DURING CRISIS

How you communicate during crisis directly impacts your team's performance, customer confidence, and stakeholder support. Strategic communication becomes as important as financial or operational decisions.

The first principle of crisis communication is radical transparency within appropriate boundaries. People can handle difficult truths delivered with clarity and context. What they cannot tolerate is sensing that information is being withheld or manipulated. Share reality honestly, including challenges and uncertainties, while maintaining confidentiality where legally required.

Timing and sequencing matter enormously. Establish communication hierarchies that respect those most directly affected by decisions. Team members should never learn critical information about their roles from external sources. Customers deserve direct notification of impacts before public announcements. Investors require updates at intervals that balance transparency against operational bandwidth.

Finding a balance between acknowledging reality and maintaining confidence requires you to carefully calibrate your message. This isn't false optimism or toxic positivity—it's grounded hope based on specific, credible response plans. When you can articulate both the problem and a plausible path forward, you have the best chance for success.

EXTERNAL STAKEHOLDER MANAGEMENT

Crisis isn't just internal. It extends to a complex network of external stakeholders, each with different needs, concerns, and potential impact on your recovery efforts. Financial partners, for example, require particularly thoughtful engagement during crisis. Whether traditional lenders, investors, or alternative financing sources, these relationships can provide crucial flexibility when managed proactively. The cardinal rule is simple but frequently violated: Never surprise them. Communicate challenges early, arrive with potential solutions rather than just problems, and maintain absolute credibility in all projections and commitments.

Suppliers and vendors represent both potential vulnerabilities and sources of assistance. If you've built genuine partnership, you might have an ally who will provide extended terms, priority fulfillment, or creative financing arrangements—but only when approached honestly and given adequate time to accommodate your needs.

When it comes to customers, key accounts deserve personalized outreach from your senior leadership with specific contingency plans. Broader customer segments need reassurance too—without unnecessarily highlighting problems that may not affect them. In all cases, maintaining service delivery builds the kind of loyalty that lasts beyond recovery.

BECOMING THE LEADER CRISIS DEMANDS

Crisis doesn't create leaders, but it inevitably reveals them. The principles and practices outlined in this chapter aren't just techniques for navigating difficulty—they're pathways for becoming the leader your organization needs precisely when that leadership matters most.

The journey begins with self-leadership—establishing the mental clarity, emotional stability, and personal resilience needed for sound decision-making under pressure. Without this foundation, even the most sophisticated crisis response strategies will fail during implementation.

It's interesting, isn't it, that the leadership required during crisis isn't fundamentally different from effective leadership during stability? You still need to build effective support systems, develop frameworks for priority setting and decision-making, be able to see the forest through the trees, and communicate strategically both internally and externally. The big difference? Leading in crisis is simply more concentrated, more consequential, and more revealing. By developing these capabilities before they're desperately needed, you create the foundation for resilience that serves in all conditions.

The legacy John left wasn't just in what he built, but in how he led, especially when the path forward wasn't clear. That same capacity for clear-minded, purpose-driven leadership lives within you. Crisis doesn't define your leadership; it merely reveals the leader you've already become through daily choices, consistent disciplines, and intentional development.

Lead yourself well, and you'll discover the capacity to lead others through whatever challenges you face—not just to survival, but to renewal and growth beyond what seemed possible in the midst of difficulty. And the good news? Opportunity sometimes lives underneath the mess that's on the surface. We'll talk more about what that is and how to uncover it in the next chapter. For now, just sit with the fact that it's likely there, that is, if you start by taking the macro view, which is what we're doing with the creation of your One Page Recovery Plan. In chapter 4, we'll start to develop just that.

MARCHING ORDERS: FIND CLARITY IN THE CHAOS

Leading yourself well isn't just good personal practice—it's the foundation of organizational resilience. It's the secret sauce that makes the One Page Recovery Plan work in the first place. The best plan in the world can't be implemented by a human being who is depleted or unable to show up fully. The disciplines, mindsets, and support systems described in this chapter create the stable platform from which all effective crisis response flows. Master these elements, and you'll find yourself capable of clarity amid chaos that others find impossible to achieve:

1. Establish a daily practice for mental clarity—whether running, meditation, prayer, or another discipline that works for you. Commit to this practice with special devotion, precisely when it feels like you don't have time for it.

2. Identify two or three trusted advisers who will tell you the truth without reservation. Explicitly ask for their commitment to candor, especially when it's uncomfortable. Create regular touchpoints with these advisers that continue regardless of business conditions.

3. Document your personal warning signs of emotional decision-making. These might include sleep disruption, irritability, catastrophic thinking, or decision paralysis. Share this list with a trusted colleague who has permission to flag these behaviors when they appear.

4. Create a personal crisis protocol for maintaining perspective. This should include specific actions you'll take when facing

significant challenges—people you'll call, questions you'll ask yourself, and boundaries you'll maintain even under pressure.

5. Practice mental distancing by regularly viewing your company through an outside lens. Schedule quarterly sessions where you examine your business as a consultant would, challenging assumptions and evaluating options without emotional attachment to past decisions.

NOTES FROM THE WAR ROOM

Your team will mirror your mental state—for better or worse. Investing in your own clarity and composure isn't selfish; it's the foundation of responsible leadership.

Developing practices that create mental clarity is essential crisis preparation. These disciplines—whether physical exercise, meditation, prayer, or reflective writing—serve as pressure release valves and perspective-restoration tools. They create the mental space needed to separate reaction from response, emotion from strategy, and urgent from important.

Your personal leadership foundation determines your organizational impact. The principles, practices, and support systems described in this chapter aren't peripheral considerations—they're central determinants of your effectiveness. Invest in them with the same seriousness you bring to financial planning, strategic development, and operational excellence.

CHAPTER 3

FACE BRUTAL FACTS WHILE MAINTAINING HOPE

ONCE, A FOUNDER I WAS WORKING WITH AND I SAT ACROSS THE table from our lender—a very nice guy who was clearly struggling to deliver an important message to us. In short, the lender was saying that we had six months to figure out a workable solution, or we would be moved to the workout group, putting us into default.

"That was a great meeting," the founder said after the lender left the room. "The bank is completely behind us. We just need to get through the next couple of months."

"Are you sure?" I questioned. "He was sent here to tell us they are planning to move us to the workout group."

I'd heard variations of this statement in nearly every turnaround situation I'd encountered. The specific details changed—sometimes it was an investor meeting, other times a potential client—but the underlying pattern remained consistent: Leaders clinging to isolated positive signals while ignoring overwhelming evidence to the contrary.

"Let's look at the balance sheet together," I suggested, keeping my tone neutral as I opened the financial statements. He reluctantly nodded, though I could sense his resistance. As we reviewed the numbers line by line, the disconnect between his perception and financial reality became increasingly apparent.

His company had over $1.2 million in past-due vendor obligations and barely enough cash to cover the next payroll. Meanwhile, their line of credit was fully maxed out. No matter how supportive his banker might have sounded, these numbers told an unambiguous story.

"Look," I said finally, "your banker may genuinely want to help, but these numbers show a company in serious distress. The balance sheet doesn't lie."

His posture changed as the reality sank in—shoulders slumping slightly as the weight of the situation registered. But what happened next revealed why facing brutal facts becomes the essential first step toward transformation.

Once he acknowledged the severity of their situation, something shifted in our conversation. Instead of wasting energy defending an untenable position, he began engaging with potential solutions. Within two hours, we'd outlined the framework for a recovery plan built on the foundation of clear-eyed assessment rather than wishful thinking. The plan wasn't easy—it involved difficult choices about staffing, services, and structure—but it was grounded in reality.

Twenty years of turnaround experience have taught me that true transformation begins with assessment—one that balances brutal honesty with practical opportunity. The balance sheet doesn't lie, but it also doesn't tell the complete story. Learning to read both the hard truth of your situation and the possibilities within it creates the foundation for everything that follows.

THE DANGER OF WISHFUL THINKING IN CRISIS

Wishful thinking when your business is on the brink creates perhaps the most dangerous leadership trap—one that appears harmless or even positive while systematically undermining effective response. Unlike obvious errors like panic or paralysis, wishful thinking feels constructive while actually delaying necessary action until options narrow and resources deplete.

What makes wishful thinking particularly dangerous is how it masquerades as legitimate hope or strategic patience. Have you ever justified continued investment in failing approaches as "persistence" or "staying the course" rather than recognizing the fundamental disconnect between their expectations and emerging reality? John and I did. We value grit, which is a necessary trait for leaders—and one that can also lead to staying the course when we should have bailed. In fact, one of The Ruhlin Way guidelines states: *Grit is critical for prolonged success, but you will lose some battles. Move on.* We had to remind ourselves that it's OK to lose once in a while and that, when it happens, move on quickly because mitigating the damage is healthier than adding more loss. I know we are not alone. This framing feels better than acknowledging missteps but prevents the course corrections necessary for survival.

The ways wishful thinking undermines effective crisis response are specific and predictable: It delays necessary but difficult decisions until financial constraints remove options that might have preserved value, misdirects limited resources toward supporting fiction rather than building from reality, and undermines team trust by creating disparities between public messaging and observable reality.

This last one matters a lot, and we'll talk about it in depth in this chapter. That's because when your leadership communications consistently contradict what team members can plainly see, your credibility erodes precisely when it becomes most essential for coordinated response. One technology company maintained outward optimism about its market position, for example, even as employees witnessed contract cancellations and declining sales. This disparity didn't just damage morale—it prevented the collective focus on reinvention that might have enabled transformation.

Distinguishing between legitimate strategic patience and wishful thinking requires brutal honesty (seeing a theme here?) about the evidence supporting your expectations.

And no, the antidote to wishful thinking isn't pessimism; it's reality-based planning that acknowledges both challenges and possibilities. This approach creates genuine pathways forward rather than fantasies that feel better temporarily but ultimately deepen crisis.

THE DIFFERENCE BETWEEN OPTIMISM AND DELUSION

Effective crisis leadership requires maintaining optimism about possibilities without sliding into delusion about realities. (Jim Collins referenced this dynamic that he calls the Stockdale Paradox in his excellent book, *Good to Great*.) This distinction isn't merely semantic—it represents your most crucial leadership capability during challenging periods.

But that doesn't mean it's easy.

Authentic optimism and dangerous delusion can appear superficially similar because they both involve positive expectations about future outcomes. However, they operate from fundamentally different relationships with present reality. Optimism acknowledges current challenges while maintaining confidence in your capability to address them, whereas delusion either denies existing challenges or assumes their resolution without credible pathways forward.

Maintaining authentic optimism when times are rough doesn't happen automatically—it requires deliberate mental discipline. The pressure of challenging circumstances naturally pushes leaders toward either excessive pessimism or compensatory delusion. Calibrating between these extremes demands regular reality-testing through trusted advisers, systematic examination of evidence, and intellectual honesty about the difference between what you hope will happen and what evidence suggests might happen.

This balanced stance—facing reality without being defined by it—creates the foundation for effective crisis response. It enables difficult decisions without despair and maintains energy without fantasy, creating the mental conditions necessary for genuine transformation rather than temporary comfort.

FINDING OPPORTUNITY WITHIN CRISIS

Crisis strips away the comfortable assumptions and established patterns that define normal operations, as we discussed in the last chapter. Here, let's go a little bit deeper. We know that while this disruption creates obvious challenges, it also reveals opportunities that remain hidden during periods of stability. But why?

In stable periods, organizations naturally develop routines that become effectively invisible—they're simply "how things are done." These patterns create efficiency but also constrain exploration of alternatives that might create greater value. Crisis shatters these constraints, forcing reconsideration of fundamental assumptions—and boom! Suddenly, there's space for possibilities previously filtered out by success-based thinking.

I experienced this dynamic vividly during the early days of Ruhlin Promotion Group and Gift·ology. John was scrappy. Tell him no, and he would figure out a way to make it possible. This trait was particularly helpful because we faced seemingly unlimited constraints: Limited cash, stabilizing but still vulnerable operation, and a model we believed in but hadn't yet proven at scale. Countless times, he would have an idea that I agreed was great, but unfortunately, we lacked the resources to see it through. Oftentimes, he would figure out a way to trade for it to happen anyway.

One time, I didn't think the idea was great, but John did, and he wouldn't let it go. Ever hear the Brooks Brothers story with Cameron Herold? John was convinced we should invest $8,000 to arrange Cameron's hotel room at the Ritz in Cleveland as a Brooks Brothers showroom. All the clothes were Cameron's size due to John's cleverness during a previous connection with Cameron. (This story is worth a read if you don't know about it.)[1] The backstory, though, is that we didn't have the money. Liz and I were funding the company during that time by not depositing checks and allowing unequal distributions to help John.

"We can do this," I told John on the way to Cleveland that day, "but if it fails, you've got to cover it through your equity account."

Guess what? It didn't fail. Ever since, Cameron has been one of our biggest advocates and has sent countless referrals for both gifting campaigns and stages.

What is the lesson here? Simple: Try *deliberately* framing constraints as innovation drivers rather than merely as limitations. Your question then shifts from "What can't we do because of these constraints?" to "What might these constraints force us to discover?"

---

1   John Ruhlin, "3 Keys to Giving Client Gifts with Maximum Impact," August 24, 2017, *https://johnruhlin.com/3-keys-to-giving-client-gifts-with-maximum-impact/*.

ASSESSING YOURSELF FIRST:
THE HARDEST QUESTIONS TO ASK

Before evaluating anyone else in your organization when it comes to their role and performance in crisis, you must begin with the most challenging assessment of all: An honest examination of your *own* leadership capabilities. This self-assessment represents perhaps the most difficult aspect of the entire evaluation process, yet it creates the foundation for everything that follows. Ask yourself a simple question: As board chair of your company (which you *are*, by the way, if you are founder), would *you* hire *you* as CEO?

The difficulty in answering this question stems from fundamental human psychology; we all maintain self-perceptions that may not align with reality, particularly around capabilities central to our identity. As leaders, we've typically achieved our positions through demonstrated competence. We're used to winning or, at the least, being able to solve problems in front of us, so we've created natural resistance to questioning that competence, even when circumstances change dramatically.

During Malone University's transformation while I served as board chair, I had to confront uncomfortable questions about my own capabilities. Did I possess the governance expertise to lead such a fundamental institutional change? Did my business background translate effectively to higher education challenges? Did I have the patience to deal with the painstakingly slow pace of higher education? These questions weren't theoretical—they directly impacted whether I should step in to lead or create space for someone better suited to our specific challenges.

The most valuable self-assessment is often the most uncomfortable. Here's what to do:

- Start by examining whether your particular strengths align with current challenges. Leaders typically possess distinctive capabilities—strategic vision, operational excellence, relationship building, financial acumen—that create value in specific contexts. Crisis often changes which capabilities matter most, potentially creating misalignment between your strengths and current needs.

- Assess your emotional capacity for the decisions ahead. Different crises demand different emotional capabilities. Turnarounds involving significant staff reductions require the emotional resilience to make difficult people decisions while maintaining empathy. Market pivots demand the emotional flexibility to abandon previously championed approaches. Honestly assessing whether you possess the specific emotional capacities required for your situation creates crucial clarity.

- Examine your attachment to past decisions that might cloud your current judgment. Leaders naturally develop investment in approaches they've initiated or championed. This attachment can create powerful resistance to necessary changes, particularly when those changes might be interpreted as acknowledging previous missteps.

The bottom line is that effective self-assessment isn't about finding fault—it's about creating alignment between leadership capabilities and current requirements. This alignment might involve several potential outcomes: Developing new capabilities to meet current challenges, bringing in complementary leadership to address gap areas, or potentially transitioning leadership entirely if the misalignment proves too significant. Honest self-assessment is why so many founders have asked me to partner with them; they recognized they didn't have the experience or capability the situation required, and they needed me to guide them. That's a courageous action.

The leaders who navigate these rough roads most effectively aren't those with unrealistic self-confidence but those with accurate self-awareness. This clarity doesn't diminish leadership effectiveness; it enhances it by creating the foundation for decisions that serve organizational needs rather than ego protection.

SIGNS YOU MIGHT BE PART OF THE PROBLEM

I've observed recurring patterns that signal when a leader might be contributing to challenges rather than driving their resolution. For me, the warning sign I pay the closest attention to is when I lack clarity. Over the years, I have experienced moments of intense clarity during very chaotic times. When I lack clarity, I pause. How about you? Do you have a warning sign you have identified as meaningful for you? Here is a list of some signs to consider. (Now, the following warning signs don't *necessarily* indicate leadership failure, but if you see yourself reflected in any of them, that certainly suggests you may benefit from an assessment or potential adjustment.)

- **Consistent defensiveness when facing challenging information:** When data contradicts your expectations or others raise concerns about direction, does your initial response focus on defending current approaches or genuinely exploring alternative perspectives?

- **Negative communication patterns with your team:** When facing challenges, do team members bring problems to you early or only when issues become unavoidable? Do they express genuine perspectives or carefully package information to align with your known preferences? Teams quickly learn which messages will be welcomed and which will trigger defensive responses. If you're hearing only comfortable information during challenging periods, your leadership approach might be filtering crucial reality.

- **Decision isolation:** Do you find yourself making increasingly consequential decisions with decreasing input from others? This pattern often begins with legitimate time pressure but evolves into a problematic leadership pattern.

- **Your relationship with external advisers:** Do you seek counsel from those who challenge your thinking or primarily those who validate existing perspectives? One clear warning sign emerges when you find yourself dismissing input from advisers who previously influenced your thinking but now present challenging perspectives. This selective receptivity often indicates defensive leadership rather than genuine information-seeking.

- **Your response to failure:** When initiatives don't produce expected results, is your primary focus finding external factors to explain disappointing outcomes, or do you readily examine your own decisions as potential contributors?

Physical and emotional patterns are also worth your examination. If you're experiencing significant disruptions in your sleep, energy, exercise, or spiritual practices, that could be a sign you are exceeding your current capabilities and need to bring in support. Don't get me wrong: Recognizing these warning signs doesn't diminish leadership—it demonstrates the self-awareness essential for effective crisis response. The most respected leaders I've worked with demonstrate remarkable candor about their own potential contributions to organizational challenges, creating the foundation for genuine transformation rather than surface-level change.

EVALUATING YOUR TEAM

After you've evaluated yourself, it's time to turn your attention to your team.

Traditional team evaluation focuses primarily on skills and experience—what people know and what they've accomplished. While these factors matter, my turnaround experience has repeatedly shown that character attributes often prove more predictive of crisis performance than technical capabilities alone. The pressure of challenging circumstances reveals deeper patterns that remain hidden during normal operations. Make it a habit to consider who you trust to be in the trenches with you.

Crisis creates distinctive conditions that test specific character attributes:

- The uncertainty of rapidly changing circumstances reveals **adaptability**—the willingness to adjust approaches rather than clinging to established methods when conditions change.

- The constraint of limited resources reveals **resourcefulness**—the capacity to accomplish objectives despite inadequate tools, information, or financial resources.

- The pressure of difficult circumstances reveals **resilience**—the ability to still thrive despite setbacks and disappointments. Crisis inevitably includes failures, false starts, and unexpected challenges that test emotional stamina.

- Crisis reveals **integrity**—consistency between stated values and actual decisions when competing priorities create difficult choices.

MESSY MOMENT: YOUR SPOUSE IS THE MOST IMPORTANT PERSON

At Gift·ology, we talk a lot about the importance of including the inner circle. John knew that if you take care of the family, everything else will take care of itself. Many of us founders say we are working so hard because we want our families to have better lives. I believe we are being authentic when we say such things, at least I know I am. But in practice it is often our families that sacrifice the most.

I have been incredibly blessed by my wife of twenty-five years, Liz. Lindsay (John's wife) jokes that she and Liz didn't understand what they signed up for when John and I combined forces. Liz has endured a lot. She moved out of a house we owned and into a duplex because I wanted to buy a company; she moved halfway across the country, leaving a job she loved; she moved into a small apartment when John and I combined forces; we lived on her income the first year John and I were together; she worked for free, shipping product every weekend to support our efforts; she has endured my habit of getting lost in my thoughts; she attends social events she doesn't necessarily enjoy; she has raised three amazing kids; and most importantly, she has remained steadfast in her belief in her savior with an incredibly strong faith.

She has done all of this with grace. If you are reading this book, there is a good chance you are in a battle right now. I pray that your spouse supports you like Liz has supported me. My warning to you (*and me*) is to acknowledge how this experience is impacting your spouse. Your role as a spouse and parent isn't on hold while you maneuver your current circumstances. Be the spouse and parent you need to be.

THE DIFFERENCE BETWEEN LOYALTY AND CAPABILITY

Loyalty and capability are not the same, nor do they carry the same weight, especially in crisis.

I've encountered this dynamic repeatedly across turnaround situations. Leaders hesitate to make necessary role changes involving long-tenured team members who demonstrate genuine commitment but lack essential capabilities for the current challenge. This hesitation stems from understandable concerns: These folks have often made significant contributions historically, demonstrated admirable value alignment, and remained steadfast through difficult periods. Consideration of their continued role feels like an evaluation of their worth, but it's not. As easy as this is to understand, it's also hard to act on.

Don't get me wrong: Loyalty deserves authentic appreciation. Individuals who have demonstrated commitment should be recognized, but this recognition can take multiple forms beyond role continuation. How about a potential transition to a position that's better aligned? How about an appropriate separation package that demonstrates respect for past contributions?

At the end of the day, this isn't personal judgment; it is practical assessment based on organizational needs during a critical period.

THE KEY DIFFERENCES BETWEEN FALSE HOPE AND GROUNDED OPTIMISM

I believe hope represents the most powerful resource for crisis transformation—it energizes action, sustains perseverance, and attracts essential support when challenges seem overwhelming. Still, not all hope functions equally. Understanding the crucial distinction between false hope and grounded optimism will help you protect against both demoralizing pessimism and dangerous delusion.

Take care: False hope and grounded optimism can appear superficially similar. Both involve positive expectations about future possibilities and provide emotional fuel for difficult journeys. However, they operate from fundamentally different relationships with current reality, creating dramatically different outcomes over time.

False hope maintains positive expectations despite contradictory evidence, typically in three ways. Consider these through the lens of your own experience or the example lens of, say, a retail founder continuing expansion despite consecutive store failures.

- **False hope selectively filters information**—amplifying confirming data while dismissing contradictory evidence. (The retail founder is focusing exclusively on isolated positive performance days and ignoring sustained pattern data.)

- **False hope relies on magical thinking about causation**—assuming positive outcomes will emerge without specific, validated pathways to them. (The retail founder "has a feeling" that their store will perform better in a different locale.)

- **False hope typically lacks specific verification mechanisms**—remaining vague about exactly how or when positive outcomes will take shape, making the belief effectively unfalsifiable. (The retail founder believes sales will improve in the future, but doesn't have a system to quantifiably measure what that improvement needs to look like in order to save the underperforming location.)

On the other hand, grounded optimism keeps those positive expectations while fully acknowledging current challenges and limitations. Rather than filtering reality to maintain comfort, it builds from comprehensive assessment toward specific improvement pathways. Here are a few key differences:

- **Grounded optimism generates specific, testable hypotheses about improvement pathways.** (Rather than general assertions that "things will improve," our retail founder creates concrete predictions: "If we implement these specific changes, we should see these measurable results within this timeframe.")

- **Grounded optimism acknowledges the reality of setbacks without abandoning overall direction.** (The retail founder treats setbacks as learning opportunities that refine future efforts rather than invalidate the overall direction.)

- **Grounded optimism focuses primarily on controllable factors while recognizing the reality of uncontrollable ones**. (The retail founder looks at the books and realizes opening a new store isn't the best solution and instead focuses on improving the controllables in her underperforming location.)

MARCHING ORDERS: TELL THE TRUTH

Facing brutal facts while maintaining hope is critical to your Go-Forward Operating Plan—something we'll work more on together in the next chapter. But first things first: Be honest with yourself. Your One Page Recovery Plan will just be words on a page if you aren't looking at the sometimes hard-to-look-at truth of your situation.

Speaking of truths, remember these:

- Facing brutal facts isn't pessimism; it's the foundation of genuine hope.

- Assessment without action doesn't matter.

- Every crisis contains the seeds of opportunity, but only if you're willing to see clearly.

- Your leadership capability must be part of your honest assessment.

It's time to put these ideas into motion. As you move forward, do the following:

- Identify three opportunities hidden within your current challenges.

- Conduct a personal leadership assessment.

- Schedule honest conversations with your key team members about the current reality of your situation and try to see what you might be missing.

NOTES FROM THE WAR ROOM

The most subtle avoidance mechanism involves substituting activity for assessment. You may feel the urge to launch new initiatives, reorganize departments, or implement technology upgrades—creating the appearance of addressing problems without first understanding their nature. What you get here is motion without progress, consuming resources that might otherwise support genuine transformation.

On top of that, many organizational cultures implicitly discourage brutal honesty, rewarding positive messaging while subtly penalizing bearers of challenging news.

Don't be one of them.

CHAPTER 4

BUILD YOUR GO-FORWARD OPERATING PLAN

ANOTHER BOARD MEETING AT MALONE UNIVERSITY HAD ENDED with the same tired solutions: "Recruit harder and cut costs." As I drove home that evening, frustration gnawed at me. For too long, we'd been circling the same recommendations while our financial situation continued to deteriorate. Despite earnest efforts from dedicated people, we seemed trapped in a cycle of diminishing returns.

The problem wasn't effort—everyone was working incredibly hard. It wasn't commitment—the board and leadership team deeply valued the institution. What struck me during that drive home was that we were fundamentally asking the wrong questions.

We had been approaching our challenges as operational problems requiring operational solutions. Recruit more students. Reduce expenses. Improve efficiency. These weren't bad objectives in themselves, but they addressed symptoms rather than underlying causes. They represented how to do things better without questioning what we should be doing in the first place. Plus, the industry of higher education was experiencing an incredibly difficult period, so it was easy to accept the current situation as our new reality without pushing back on that assumption.

To be very honest, I began questioning why I agreed to be board chair. I had enough on my plate with our companies and a young family, but I care deeply about Malone. Fortunately, one of my first decisions as chair, in collaboration with the president and the governance chair, was to reorient how the board operates. We needed to become more nimble.

The benefits of this decision paid off quickly. The new structure allowed me to create task forces and select whichever of the trustees (there were thirty at the time) I felt would be most impactful. Together with the president, we created a Malone of the Future Task Force, and we selected six trustees with the experience and pedigree needed to explore some tough questions. Who are we as an institution? What distinctive value do we offer? Whom do we serve most effectively? Why should students choose us over other options? These weren't operational questions but existential ones—questions about purpose and identity that we had carefully avoided while focusing on tactical improvements.

Over the next six months, we met monthly for hours. But as we engaged these questions honestly, we discovered something profound: There was a growing disconnect between our stated identity and our actual operations. We were created to serve the Church through education, but were we? We soon realized that many in our target market of the faith community no longer considered us a viable higher education option—a big problem.

Given that one of the main priorities of the board is to set direction, we called a special board meeting in July of that year for the purpose of answering a simple question: *Who is Malone?* We had 100 percent participation in that meeting with trustees from all over the country attending, and we left aligned with a unanimous vote: We exist to serve the Church, and we will be fully aligned with the faith and practice of the Evangelical Friends Church, Eastern Region (EFCER). From that day on, "win with the Church" became my battle cry.

The transformation wasn't easy or immediate, but it shifted our entire trajectory. Financial metrics improved not because we simply squeezed harder on the same operations, but because we realigned our activities with our purpose. The experience taught me a crucial lesson about crisis transformation: Before fixing operations, you must clarify purpose.

WHY CRISIS OFTEN REVEALS
A DISCONNECT FROM CORE PURPOSE

Crisis rarely strikes organizations with crystal clear purpose alignment and decisive execution. More commonly, crisis emerges precisely because disconnection from core purpose has allowed a gradual drift toward unsustainable positions. What appears initially as financial distress, operational dysfunction, or market rejection may reflect deeper misalignment between what the organization does and what actually creates distinctive value.

Sound familiar? This pattern appears consistently across industries:

- A software company gradually expands its offering to include fifteen modules across disparate business functions. Only three of these modules commanded premium pricing and customer loyalty; the others merely created complexity without corresponding value.

- A professional services firm expands into eight disciplinary areas despite having recognized expertise in only two.

- A manufacturing company diversifies into consumer products despite its distinctive capabilities residing entirely in industrial applications.

In each case, the path to crisis involved well-intentioned expansion beyond core purpose. These organizations hadn't failed at execution but had succeeded at executing activities misaligned with their fundamental value proposition. Crisis merely revealed the accumulated consequences of this misalignment.

But there's good news! Ever hear the phrase "never waste a crisis"? There is truth in that statement. Crisis creates the conditions for purpose rediscovery in a few ways:

- Financial pressure forces prioritization discussions that might otherwise remain theoretical. When resources permit the continued funding of misaligned activities, your organization can avoid confronting purpose questions. Constraint eliminates this luxury.

- Marketplace rejection provides unfiltered feedback about where distinctive value actually resides. Customers or clients vote with their choices, revealing the gap between organizational self-perception and market reality.

- Crisis creates permission for fundamental questioning that might seem disruptive during stable periods.

Understanding this pattern—that crisis may reveal purpose disconnection rather than merely operational deficiency—creates the foundation you need to move forward.

THE CRITICAL QUESTIONS THAT CLARIFY PURPOSE

Rediscovering organizational purpose amid crisis requires moving beyond general mission statements toward specific questions that reveal actual identity and distinctive contribution.

I don't consider myself an expert on discovering organizational purpose, but I have a friend who is. I recommend Robert Glazer if you feel you need more help in this area. Stay tuned for his new book, *The Compass Within: A Little Story About the Values That Guide Us.*

For our purposes of *this* book you're reading now (thanks for that, by the way), I've found that the following questions consistently create clarity about fundamental purpose that general discussions often miss:

- **Who do we serve most effectively?** Rather than aspirational statements about potential customers or clients, this question examines where your organization has actually created the most meaningful value. Here's another way to say it: Who is happy to pay us for our services?

- **What problem do we solve better than readily available alternatives?** Crisis often reveals that organizations have been competing in areas where they lack meaningful differentiation while undervaluing their most distinctive capabilities.

- **Why would someone choose us if they understood all available options?** This question moves beyond marketing claims to examine genuine competitive advantage from the customer perspective.

- **What capabilities make our organization unique?** Purpose-aligned recovery plans build from existing organizational strengths rather than aspirational capabilities. With Gift·ology after John's passing, this assessment highlighted our accumulated expertise in relationship-centered growth strategies beyond John's individual capabilities. This clarity guided our pivot toward membership offerings that leveraged this organizational knowledge rather than attempting to replicate John's unique speaking presence.

- **What higher aim gives meaning to our work beyond financial outcomes?** Effective purpose statements connect daily activities with meaningful contribution that transcends metrics alone. This connection becomes particularly important during crisis, when financial pressures might otherwise drive shortsighted decisions that compromise long-term sustainability. For Malone University, reconnecting with our founding commitment to developing faithful leaders across vocations created meaning that purely operational improvements couldn't provide.

These questions create foundation for purpose clarity by moving beyond general aspirations toward specific identity anchored in organizational reality.

THE POWER OF MACRO-LEVEL THINKING

As we've learned and as you probably know from experience, crisis naturally draws leaders toward operational details. Sensing existential threat, the understandable impulse involves addressing every visible problem, reviewing every significant decision, and personally directing critical activities. This micromanagement impulse seems intuitive—if everything matters, surely nothing can be delegated, right?

Wrong.

I know because I fell into this trap early in my career while leading a retail operation, gradually slipping into the very micromanagement trap I knew to avoid. Honestly, I think it is just easier sometimes to "do something" rather than take time to think strategically. We all started companies because we are "doers," so we naturally can fall back into "doing." I'm proof you can overcome this tendency with intentional and focused effort—and overcome, you must, because the micromanagement of details can cause distinct problems that compromise recovery prospects.

Why? Because micromanagement during crisis creates leadership bandwidth constraints precisely when strategic clarity becomes most essential, and it undermines the team engagement essential for sustainable recovery. When leaders demonstrate lack of trust through excessive operational involvement, team members naturally decrease their own initiative and ownership.

At the end of the day, organizations that navigate crisis most effectively maintain a clear distinction between strategic direction (where senior leadership adds distinctive value) and operational execution (where teams with relevant context typically make better decisions). This distinction doesn't reflect absentee leadership but rather disciplined focus on the level where leadership contribution creates greatest value—establishing clear direction, securing necessary resources, and developing talent rather than directing daily activities.

Maintaining this distinction requires both clear structural boundaries and significant personal discipline. In other words, resist the natural impulse toward operational involvement, even if you have genuine concern about execution quality. Now, this restraint doesn't indicate decreased commitment. Instead, it serves as a recognition that strategic clarity combined with appropriate operational autonomy creates a more effective crisis response than even the most well-intentioned micromanagement.

HOW TO RISE ABOVE THE OPERATIONAL NOISE

Moving from operational detail to strategic direction requires specific practices that counter your natural gravitation toward microinvolvement. There are several approaches that are particularly effective for maintaining macro-level focus:

- **Guard your capacity for strategic thinking**. Consider implementing the "40/40/20 rule"—designating 40 percent of the founder's time for external perspective-gathering (customer conversations, market analysis, competitive assessment), 40 percent for organizational direction-setting (team alignment, resource allocation decisions, priority clarification), and only 20 percent for operational involvement. This helps create structural protection against the very real desire to "fix everything all at once."

- **Create physical separation that reinforces the difference between strategic and operational focus.** During the Pennsylvania turnaround, I established dedicated time

in a separate location specifically for strategic assessment—
literally removing myself from operational environments to
create mental space for directional thinking.

- **Filter information to prevent drowning in detail—
without losing awareness.** With Gift·ology after John's
passing, we created distinct information streams—weekly
operational metrics reviewed by team leaders with excep-
tion-only reporting to me, combined with weekly strategic
indicators that received my direct attention.

MESSY MOMENT: SOMETIMES YOU JUST GET LUCKY

Prior to John and I combining forces, I was leading a challenging turnaround of several operating companies. One of
the companies was a trucking company that hauled debris
from large East Coast cities to Midwest landfills. The trucking industry includes several regulations and reporting
requirements when operating in multiple states.

We were notified by one of the regulatory agencies that
we were selected for an audit. I asked around to see what
this meant and was told it wasn't a big deal as long as your
records backed up what we reported. Great. I asked the team
for the records and was told we didn't keep records because
the founder believed information could be used against us.

Not great.

I then found out that we should expect some large fines
should the audit not go well.

Extra not great, especially because we were already in a
tough spot, which is why I was there in the first place. Large
fines could be a death blow.

We stalled the audit as long as possible. We hired an intern for an entire summer to recreate each truck's routes for the audit period and the miles driven per state using billing records, maintenance records, and Google Maps. In the end, our master spreadsheet was within 85 percent of the reporting we had submitted.

We were nervous as the scheduled time for the audit approached. When the auditor arrived, we explained what happened, what steps we took to recreate the routes, and shared the results. Turns out, this was the auditor's last audit before he quit the job he hated. He could not have cared less.

He blessed our effort, and we lived to fight another day.

YOUR KEY ECONOMIC DRIVER FORMULA: DISTINGUISHING BETWEEN WHAT MATTERS AND WHAT DOESN'T

Crisis is a time of information overload: Financial indicators flash warning signals. Team members express diverse concerns. Customers communicate changing expectations. Competitors make unexpected moves. Attempting to address everything simultaneously typically results in diffused effort that leads to zero—or, in the worst cases, negative—progress.

The specific factors that truly matter vary across organizations but typically cluster around primary economic drivers, distinctive competitive capabilities, and critical relationship assets. How do you determine the key economic driver(s)? Let's take a look at your **Key Economic Driver Formula** to find out.

But first (and not surprisingly, by now), let's assess the macro: Why is this important? One of my primary goals when I work with an organization is to reduce volatility because it is very difficult to produce consistent profits when key contributors are not predictable. When I begin working with a new partner, I focus on quickly identifying the most impactful metric to transform our economic future.

At the most basic level, I look for two things:

1. What products or services do our customers happily pay us for?

2. Of those products or services, which are our most profitable *and* which are supported by predictable revenue and scalable cost centers?

The services identified are going to become an anchor point for our turnaround effort. This is very important. In fact, if I am unable to identify services that meet these criteria, then I wouldn't have agreed to partner with the founder. Why? Because I have found that consistency is the greatest economic indicator of prolonged success.

Here's an example of this in action: After John's passing, our assessment at Gift·ology revealed that while our speaking engagements generated significant visibility, our membership community represented our most scalable and sustainable business model. This clarity enabled us to concentrate resources toward accelerated community development rather than attempting to replicate John's unique speaking presence, focusing attention where it created greatest long-term value rather than diffusing effort across multiple recovery approaches.

MY APPROACH: "I FOCUS ON THE MACRO— THE TEAM HANDLES THE MICRO"

Throughout my turnaround experiences, I've developed a specific leadership approach that's proven consistently effective during crisis: "I focus on the macro, the team handles the micro." This division creates both strategic clarity and operational effectiveness that diffused leadership typically fails to achieve.

This approach emerged from necessity rather than theory. During the Pennsylvania turnaround involving multiple struggling business units, the operational complexity exceeded what any individual could effectively manage. I quickly recognized that attempting detailed involvement across all businesses would create superficial engagement without meaningful impact. Instead, I established clear parameters around financial performance, customer satisfaction metrics, and implementation timelines while delegating specific operational approaches to business unit leaders within those boundaries.

It worked. The units where I maintained clear macro-level focus without micro-intervention showed significantly stronger recovery trajectories than those where circumstances required my operational involvement.

With John at Gift·ology, this approach became particularly valuable given our complementary capabilities. Rather than trying to redirect his natural relationship-building orientation toward operational details, I focused on creating clear directional boundaries—what we called "bumper bowling" for his entrepreneurial energy. Within these guardrails, his distinctive capabilities flourished without creating the operational chaos that might have resulted from completely unconstrained activity.

ALL ABOUT YOUR ONE PAGE RECOVERY PLAN

It's the moment you've been waiting for: Let's get down to the business of your One Page Recovery Plan.

But before we go there, you might be wondering: *Wait, I get the value of simplicity, but why just one page?* Here's why: As challenges mount, planning efforts often expand. While likely well-intentioned, this can create confusion . . . which ultimately kills execution. Clarity at the top will create clarity for your teams.

One page is the answer. Simple is the answer. But, as we know, simple doesn't necessarily mean easy. Let me tell you a little story about how I learned the value of the One Page.

THE CONDENSING CHALLENGE (AND REWARD)

During college, I faced an instructional challenge that ultimately influenced my approach to organizational planning. A professor of classes known to be difficult assigned three challenging political philosophy books per term, with just two exams: A midterm and final. The exams were blue book exams with one question for each book. (Those of you old enough to be in college in the nineties know what a blue book exam is. Fail an exam, and fail the class.)

How do you study an entire book? Well, I developed a specific approach: Distilling each book's essential content onto a single page that captured its fundamental concepts without losing critical meaning. For each text, I would read the book and highlight what I thought was important. Then I would write all the parts I highlighted into a notebook. Then, I would force myself to summarize all the notes onto one page. This helped me identify core frameworks, key principles, and illustrative examples that demonstrated central concepts. Rather than attempting to retain every detail, I concentrated on fundamentals. Then, during exam time, I memorized three pages of notes while my classmates were studying books. It worked, and I received A's in all his classes. The results, as you likely guessed, proved instructive beyond college. I discovered that this condensing process actually enhanced my understanding rather than compromising it. The discipline it took to identify essentials helped me deepen my comprehension rather than focusing only on retention. Plus, at the end of it, I had a handy tool to reference.

This experience directly influenced my approach to crisis planning. When organizations face existential challenges, they typically don't suffer from insufficient information or inadequate analysis. Rather, they struggle with converting abundant knowledge into focused action that creates meaningful momentum. The One Page Recovery Plan forces ruthless prioritization—and it's worth it.

REMINDER: THE CRITICAL ELEMENTS THAT MUST APPEAR ON YOUR ONE PAGE RECOVERY PLAN

You'll recall at the beginning of this book, I gave a macro view (go figure, right?) of what your One Page Recovery Plan should include. Now, let's get a little more specific:

- Every effective one-page plan includes a **clear purpose statement** that connects recovery activities with organizational identity. This isn't merely inspirational language; it guides your actions. During Gift·ology's transformation after John's passing, our purpose clarity around "helping leaders love on their relationships because everything rises and falls on relationships" provided essential context for specific recovery priorities.

- The specific articulation of **three to five strategic priorities from your Go-Forward Operating Plan** (chapter 4). Using Gift·ology as an example, we needed to replace the revenue generated from John's keynote presentations and high-level consulting. Years prior to John's passing, our team started developing key programs that would not require John, literally calling them "John Not Needed." Although it's very painful to think of now, this effort resulted in key programs being developed when we needed them most. One of those services is R.I.C.H. Relationship Society, which is a membership program teaching members how to build a referral network to grow their businesses just like John did.[2] Mission 600 is one of our most important strategic priorities because six hundred members replaces the anticipated revenue loss. Also, remember the Key Economic Driver Formula? Bonus: Our membership program also has predictable revenue and scalable cost centers!

- The specific articulation of **two to four financial priorities from your Go-Forward Financial Plan** (chapter 5). Staying with our Gift·ology plan as an example, I needed to be able to fund the transition to our new programs. Using the Founders Math Hack (which you will learn about shortly), I quickly realized that Gift·ology would remain profitable if I were able to unencumber the income needs of John and me from the company. This would allow our team to stay intact and provide the runway needed to successfully transition to our future. This resulted in a financial priority of Lindsay (John's wife) and me committing to support our families outside Gift·ology for at least two years.

2   John Ruhlin, *Beyond Gift·ology: Earn Endless Word of Mouth with a System That Turns Relationships into Referral Partners* (Lioncrest Publishing, 2025).

- The specific articulation of **two to four team priorities from your Go-Forward Team Plan** (chapter 6). Last, one of the major impacts of losing John was that a majority of our leads were generated by John from the stage. Without John speaking, where would our new leads come from for our "done for you" gifting strategy and campaigns? We need our Gift·ologist team, led by Kami and Carissa, to generate new leads through referral relationships, so one of our team priorities is to use our Referral Partner Transformation course to develop a referral network. Truly, we are eating our own dog food, as the saying goes.

While the fundamental principles of one-page planning remain consistent across contexts, effective implementation requires thoughtful adaptation for different industries, organizational sizes, and specific challenges. This adaptation doesn't change the essential elements; it simply adjusts their expression. I have used One Page Plans for recovery efforts in technology companies, retail companies, a university board, and (of course) Gift·ology.

I want to note that the one-page planning approach isn't my original creation. While I've adapted and refined it through multiple turnarounds, its fundamental concepts build from work by Vern Harnish, founder of the Entrepreneurs' Organization (EO), who developed structured approaches for maintaining strategic focus within growing companies facing increasing complexity.

Harnish's insight—that organizations require extraordinary discipline to maintain clear direction amid growing operational detail—provided the foundation for approaches that I've subsequently tailored specifically for crisis application. His emphasis on "less is more" when establishing strategic priorities, combined with rigorous implementation accountability, directly influenced the frameworks I've applied across diverse turnaround situations—and I'm forever grateful.

THE FOUNDER'S MATH HACK

Another tool in your crisis toolbox is the Founder's Math Hack—and this one, like the One Page Recovery Plan, is really important. But first, I get it: Traditional financial reporting typically creates more confusion than clarity for founders. While comprehensive statements provide necessary information for detailed analysis, their structure often is hard to sort through and swallows up the vital few factors that actually disproportionately influence outcomes.

If you're thinking, *I need a tool to simplify financial reporting to easily model the factors that will create the greatest impact. I need to know where to focus my time, energy, and attention to produce the greatest return*, then what you need is the Founder's Math Hack. The long and short of it is that simplified financial frameworks like this one accelerate your decision-making capabilities while maintaining macro perspective on fundamental trajectory. Additionally, the Founder's Math Hack provides clarity on the impact of the operating priorities determined critical in your One Page Recovery Plan. For example, I used a Founders Math Hack for Gift·ology to quickly determine the targets required for us to replace the revenue I expected to lose when John passed away. This information led to the plan we titled Mission 600. It was also useful in determining the funding required for us to successfully implement our plan. For us, creating simplified understanding provided immediate clarity. Were there a lot of unanswered questions about our plan? Of course! But I understood clearly what we needed to accomplish from a macro view, and that clarity provides confidence: Both in your own mind and for those you lead.

In this section, we'll explore the Founder's Math Hack together. In the next chapter, we'll look at it as part of your Go-Forward Financial Plan. Additionally, you can find a sample application of this tool in appendix B.

IDENTIFYING THE ONLY NUMBERS THAT TRULY MATTER TO YOUR BUSINESS

Effective financial leadership during crisis requires distinguishing between the vital few metrics that drive organizational performance and the many figures that create complexity. That said, I've found that most businesses can focus on remarkably few numbers while maintaining a big picture understanding of financial trajectory.

How? Begin by identifying your organization's critical economic drivers—the specific factors that disproportionately influence sustainable financial performance. (Hint: Use the Key Economic Driver Formula referenced earlier in this chapter.) For all the technology companies I partnered with, for example, I learned that agreement (subscription) revenue relative to fixed operational costs determined sustainable profitability more significantly than any other factor. While their financial statements contained hundreds of individual metrics, this fundamental relationship between predictable revenue and operational structure created the foundation for all other financial outcomes.

Beyond core economic drivers, crisis focus requires clear understanding of the specific indicators that reveal emerging problems *before* they become catastrophic. For most organizations, these early warning metrics include cash conversion cycle (how quickly investment in operations returns as available cash) and fixed-cost coverage through predictable revenue sources. These indicators most often provide advance notice of challenges while you still have time to adjust proactively—before you get to crisis stage.

Here are the three common metrics that typically provide essential clarity, regardless of your industry:

- **The cash conversion cycle**—the time required for investment in operations to return as available cash—provides fundamental insight into financial sustainability regardless of reported profitability. This metric combines receivable collection periods, inventory holding time, and payment timing into a robust understanding of organizational liquidity dynamics.

- **The relationship between predictable revenue and fixed operational costs** reveals fundamental business sustainability more clearly than traditional profit calculations. Organizations with predictable revenue streams (subscriptions, agreements, contracts) covering fixed operational costs maintain stability during market fluctuations that creates both survival capacity during downturns and investment capability during opportunities. Let's look at this in action: A technology company transformed their vulnerability by progressively increasing agreement revenue coverage of fixed costs from 65 percent to 95 percent—creating resilience that enabled strategic choices rather than reactive decisions during subsequent market disruption.

- **The working capital requirements relative to operational scale** provides essential insight into growth sustainability regardless of current profitability. This relationship reveals whether expansion will require proportionate capital investment or enable increasing returns through operational leverage.

In a moment, we'll examine a big picture case study and put this all into practice.

A FOUNDER'S MATH HACK CASE STUDY: AGREEMENT REVENUE VERSUS FIXED COSTS

One technology company's transformation particularly illustrates the power of simplified financial understanding. When I began working with them, they faced a rapidly deteriorating cash position. They were losing significant money consistently despite generating millions of dollars in revenue because their fundamental economic driver, agreement revenue (subscription services with predictable monthly billing) relative to fixed operational costs (the expenses required to maintain core business operations regardless of transaction volume), was far too low. This gap created a structural deficit, resulting in income volatility because nonagreement revenue is inconsistent.

This simplified understanding provided a degree of clarity for the founder that traditional financial analysis had failed to provide. Our solution was simple, albeit difficult to execute: We targeted expense reductions to achieve an agreement-revenue-to-fixed-cost target of 80 percent. We concentrated fixed-cost reductions on expenses that didn't impact service delivery to our client base. Next, we only accepted nonagreement revenue projects from clients whom we supported monthly with an agreement. This reduced our volatility, and we consistently generated earnings and operating cash. We made these changes over a weekend, and we were cash positive in forty-five days! That's the power of simplified understanding. Executing the changes was not easy nor pleasant, but the path was clear.

Within twelve months, they increased agreement revenue coverage of fixed costs to 92 percent—creating foundational stability that enabled strategic choices rather than reactive decisions. This improvement came through both expanding existing client subscriptions and converting transaction-based relationships to agreement structures that provided mutual benefit through predictability. Their operational changes focused specifically on creating delivery capacity that scaled more efficiently with transaction volume, enabling profitable handling of variable business without compromising core service quality.

BASE HITS VERSUS HOME RUNS AND THE DANGER OF BETTING ON BIG WINS

Crisis often creates temptation toward "home run" solutions—transformative initiatives that might dramatically change trajectory if successful, but carry significant execution risk and resource requirements. While these approaches occasionally succeed, "base hit" strategies—focused initiatives with higher implementation probability and faster feedback cycles—typically create more sustainable recovery despite their apparently incremental nature.

The superiority of "base hit" approaches is evident: They typically generate earlier feedback and allow for rapid adjustment, create progressive momentum and confidence, and distribute risk as a way to hedge your bets. I often tell founders that we are going to set our plan and allocate resources to produce base hits.

In the process, if we hit a home run, then we get to celebrate a grand slam!

MARCHING ORDERS: YOUR TURN

Now that you understand the components of your Go-Forward Operating Plan and where the One Page Recovery Plan fits in, it's time to put your energy into your own. Here's what's next:

- In appendix A, you'll find Gift·ology's One Page Recovery Plan. Use it as a template to get you started.

- Using the Key Economic Driver Formula, identify your service offerings that will anchor your recovery plan.

- Add the top three to five operational priorities to your One Page Recovery Plan.

- Identify the four key metrics for your organization as they relate to the Founder's Math Hack, referring to the explanations and examples in this chapter.

- Be strategic, but don't overthink this: Develop a "parking lot" for ideas that don't align with immediate priorities, and rest assured that you can revisit those when you have the bandwidth.

NOTES FROM THE WAR ROOM

As you go about creating your Go-Forward Operating Plan, remember that it must reconnect with your core purpose before addressing tactics. Don't skip this step. Doing so is a common trap for leaders in crisis. Remember: Simplicity and clarity matter more than comprehensiveness, and systems should leverage the founder's strength rather than trying to fix weaknesses.

Your financial understanding requires your utmost focus on the few metrics that actually gas your engine. In the next chapter, we'll look more into that in particular as you build your Go-Forward Financial Plan.

Buckle up!

CHAPTER 5

BUILD YOUR GO-FORWARD FINANCIAL PLAN

WHEN I FIRST SAW THE FINANCIAL STATEMENTS, MY HEART SANK. The company had exactly thirty days of runway left—one month before they'd be completely out of cash.

I remember walking into their office that morning. The founders' desks had family photos—young children smiling back at their parents, who were now staring at financial oblivion. Those images hit me hard. This wasn't just about saving a business; it was about preserving livelihoods, supporting families, and protecting dreams.

I've been in this position more times than I care to count. Financial crisis creates a particular kind of pressure that can cloud judgment exactly when clarity is most needed. It's easy to panic, to grasp at quick fixes, or to simply freeze.

But over twenty years in the trenches has taught me that even the direst financial situations can be transformed with the right approach. For this (and every) company, this meant first understanding the brutal facts, then developing a targeted plan that would extend their runway while we implemented bigger structural changes.

By Wednesday of that week, we had developed a framework that would give us breathing room. We identified over $300,000 in immediate cost reductions. We centered our growth strategy on their key economic drivers and focused the reductions in other areas, elevated the founder's spouse (a very talented administrator and trained programmer) to oversee operations while focusing the founder on building sales networks, and managed cash with discipline to build liquidity and improve our financial health. Most critically, we communicated clearly and candidly with our team and key stakeholders.

What happened next is what I've seen repeatedly across multiple turnarounds: When you face financial reality directly and implement systematic solutions, seemingly impossible situations become manageable. The company didn't just survive—eighteen months later, they were more profitable than they'd ever been.

The financial principles we applied weren't unique to their situation. They're the same fundamentals I've used in every turnaround, principles that focus on liquidity, simplicity, and sustainability. These aren't theoretical concepts—they're battle-tested approaches that work in real situations with real companies facing real financial pressure. How do I know they work? Because I have experienced the results. Our partners have experienced at least 2.5-times profit increases in three years or less. Most produce significantly more, with one partner profitability increased six times in two years and was sold in three years.

THE REALITY OF FINANCIAL CRISIS

Let's be crystal clear about something fundamental: All companies fail for the same reason—they run out of cash.

Not most companies.

All of them.

This might seem obvious, but I've observed many leaders who don't grasp this basic truth. They fixate on profitability while ignoring cash flow, or they focus on growth while disregarding the balance sheet. I know when someone doesn't understand finances when the first thing they do is skip past the balance sheet to look at the profit and loss statement.

Financial statements tell a story, but many leaders only read the last chapter. They jump to the bottom line of the P&L and ask, "Did we make money or lose money this month?" That's an important question, but it's not nearly enough.

It is possible for profitable companies to go out of business. Let that sink in for a moment. You can show a profit on paper and still fail if you can't convert that profit to cash or manage your obligations. I've lived this reality; one company I was running generated substantial profit but struggled every month because we were carrying over six months of trade debt to our vendors from previous financial sins.

On the other hand, I've worked with companies that were unprofitable for periods but survived and eventually thrived because they managed their cash position masterfully. The balance sheet—not just the P&L—is where financial reality lives.

This misunderstanding leads to the psychology of financial denial I've seen in countless founders. They cling to positive metrics—growing revenue, increasing market share, expanding customer base—while ignoring the warning signs that really matter: Dwindling cash reserves, extending payables, and recurring cash crunches.

Like many companies I've worked with, the one we explored at the beginning of this chapter was on the brink and lost in the details of the mess. They needed a concrete plan to execute. The founder is brilliant technically, but the situation called for different skills. Like John, he was humble and trusted my instincts and direction. We confronted their financial fundamentals and executed on a plan with consistent and disciplined action. Over ten years later, we have consistently grown—and, as of this writing, we are acquiring a company that is in a similar situation he was in ten years ago. Without solid financial principles in place, his reality today would be very different.

FROM THEORY TO APPLICATION: THE FOUNDER'S MATH HACK

In reality, the organizations facing existential challenges typically fail not just because they're unprofitable but because they lack liquidity to weather disruption or manage obligations. Read that again if you have to. Understanding this distinction will help inform your next move. As for that next move, you'll be better off not just *knowing* the Founder's Math Hack, which we explained broadly in chapter 4, but *applying* it.

Remember: This tool is to help you cut through the complexity—complexity that doesn't just create confusion but that can also paralyze decision-making. When you can't clearly see the connection between your actions and your financial outcomes, you either freeze or make decisions based on incomplete information. Neither serves you well during a crisis.

The Founder's Math Hack is not about dumbing down finance; it's about creating clarity that drives action. The approach distills your entire financial picture down to the few variables that truly matter to your specific business.

Instead of focusing on every line item in your financial statements, it's time to identify your key economic drivers—the services or products your customers happily pay you for and the cost centers required to deliver them. As you learned in the last chapter, I focus on the ones where customers are happily paying you and where the revenue is predictable and cost centers are scalable. For example, with an MSP (managed service provider), I separate agreement revenue (recurring, predictable monthly fees) from project revenue (variable, unpredictable one-time work). The agreement revenue is the foundation—it's what you can build reliable cost structures around.

For Gift·ology, we identified that John on stage and consulting services were our highest profitability drivers, while the gifting services everyone associated us with were actually our least profitable offering. However, "John on stage" is not scalable, whereas R.I.C.H. Relationship Society and gifting services *are*. This clarity allowed us to make strategic decisions about where to invest our time and resources.

Remember from chapter 4 that the power of the Founder's Math Hack is that it creates a simplified model of your business that you can actually use to make decisions. It lets you see clearly how changes in a few key variables will affect your overall financial picture. Instead of being overwhelmed by dozens of metrics, you focus on the critical few that drive everything else.

For the business on the brink at the beginning of this chapter, this approach was transformative. Instead of trying to cut costs across the board, we identified their key economic drivers and protected those areas while making deeper cuts elsewhere. We restructured their pricing model to emphasize recurring revenue over project work. Within three months, their financial clarity had improved dramatically, and with it, their decision-making.

This isn't just a crisis tool—it's an ongoing discipline that creates financial clarity in good times and bad. The companies that emerge strongest from financial crisis are those that maintain this clarity long after the immediate pressure has passed.

BUILDING LIQUIDITY BEFORE REDUCING DEBT

One of the most counterintuitive lessons I've learned in multiple turnarounds is this: When facing financial crisis, building liquidity matters more than paying down debt.

This goes against the instincts of most founders, who feel moral pressure to pay down obligations as quickly as possible. The thought process is understandable: "We owe this money. We should pay it back as soon as we can." But this approach often leads to cash flow pressure that can sink an otherwise salvageable company.

I think of liquidity as your company's ability to take a punch. Without adequate cash reserves, even minor disruptions can become existential threats. A delayed payment from a major client, an unexpected equipment failure, or a sudden market shift can push a cash-starved company over the edge. Plus, you have to generate your own liquidity. In my experience, banks will not rescue you.

How much liquidity is enough? My rule of thumb is six months of fixed costs. This provides sufficient buffer to absorb shocks while giving you time to implement broader strategic changes. For companies with predictable recurring revenue, you can adjust this calculation to your fixed costs minus your agreement revenue, multiplied by six.

This approach saved the company we've been discussing in this chapter. Rather than directing their limited cash toward debt reduction, we built a liquidity reserve first. This gave us breathing room to negotiate with creditors from a position of relative strength rather than desperation. It allowed us to make strategic decisions rather than just reacting to the next crisis.

How do you build liquidity when you are in a crisis? The answer is simple and yet very hard: Execute your One Page

Recovery Plan. Your operational plan will generate positive operating cash flow; your financial plan will provide the runway. Use the resources generated to build liquidity while you maintain consistent payments to your creditors, without fail. While this may only marginally reduce your total amount owed, in my experience, creditors ultimately work with you if you are consistent and communicate. Once you meet your liquidity targets, ease down your obligations to your creditors over time. This requires extreme discipline, but you will be thankful you followed the plan. Trust me.

At the end of the day, nothing is linear, and your company must be able to take a punch as quickly as possible. I've seen this pattern repeatedly. In nearly every turnaround, there will be an unforeseen event that will either be your end or another story to tell. For example, one technology company we partnered with experienced a very serious failure with their data storage systems following our turnaround effort. The consequences were company-threatening. Fortunately, we had adequate liquidity to move forward quickly, and the disciplined habits that were developed during our turnaround paid additional dividends while we successfully maneuvered through another crisis.

This principle extends beyond crisis situations. Companies with strong balance sheets can weather downturns that destroy their competitors. They can seize opportunities when others can't. They can make decisions based on long-term value rather than short-term pressure.

The balance sheet is where financial strength lives. P&L problems are relatively easy to fix—you can adjust pricing, reduce expenses, or change your sales strategy. Balance sheet problems are much harder to solve. By prioritizing liquidity, you create the foundation for sustainable financial health.

THE TAX PLANNING HACK

One of the most powerful but least discussed financial tools for postrecovery companies is what I call the Tax Planning Hack. It's not a system—it's definitely a hack—and it's something I use for visibility in a simplified way.

Let's start with a warning: You will need to account for tax obligations as you recover. Trust me. I learned this the hard way. Oftentimes, founders won't owe tax estimates because they likely didn't generate earnings the years before we partnered together. Once we are generating significant earnings, tax payments become a cash burden to manage. I failed to account for tax obligations during my first turnaround. We made substantial profits the first year, and while I knew taxes would be owed, I failed to account for the amount. The result was a wiping out of the liquidity we'd worked so far to build. Lesson learned. From then on, I built tax obligations into the cash planning efforts—an experience that led me to create this hack.

At the end of the day, the road to financial health is filled with potholes, and the Tax Planning Hack helps keep the road as smooth as possible.

Here's the concept: As you generate earnings, you accrue tax obligations throughout the year based on a set percentage of earnings. (I used 40 percent most times, but it depends on your circumstances.) That first year, you will owe very little tax, so your accrual will grow significantly. This creates an opportunity to use these funds as working capital in the interim, as long as you're disciplined about setting them aside when payment comes due.

I use a virtual escrow approach. In my accounting system, I create a separate account for tax obligations. As we generate profits that will create tax liabilities, I allocate that money to the virtual account—but only in the accounting system and not in the bank. I know exactly how much we'll owe and when, but until that payment date arrives, I can use those funds as part of our working capital. Then when tax payments are due, I transfer the funds from the virtual account in the accounting system. This creates complete visibility in a simplified way. I understand what our operating cash is in reality, but I also understand what our tax obligations are. This visibility prevents the all-too-common surprise when tax bills come due. The same process works post-recovery as your earnings levels continue to grow year over year.

To be crystal clear: I'm not suggesting you neglect tax obligations or use these funds for speculative purposes. The discipline of this approach is that you maintain absolute clarity about what portion of your cash belongs to the tax authorities and when it needs to be paid. It is important to note that these funds are also not included in the liquidity targets we discussed previously.

This approach has helped numerous companies I've worked with extend their runway during difficult periods.

What makes this hack particularly powerful is that it's entirely legitimate when done properly. You're simply managing the timing of payments while maintaining complete transparency about your obligations. This is definitely not part of generally accepted accounting principles (GAAP), so accountants likely won't offer this plan. That's why it's a hack. But it works. And for founders navigating financial challenges, this disciplined approach to tax planning can be a crucial tool for creating breathing room.

RUNWAY ASSESSMENT AND EXTENSION

Understanding exactly how much runway you have—how long you can operate before running out of cash—is perhaps the most fundamental financial calculation for companies in crisis. Yet

I'm consistently surprised by how few leaders can answer this question with precision.

Here's my framework for calculating runway:

- **Establish your timeline.** How long will it take to implement your One Page Recovery Plan and begin generating positive cash flow? For our example organization, this meant determining how long it would take to cut costs, implement pricing changes, and complete one accounts receivable cycle. Our estimate was forty-eight days.

- **Estimate your liquidity.** What cash do you have on hand, and what are your firm cash receipts during this timeline? For our example organization, they had zero cash on hand but expected $360,000 in collections during our forty-eight-day window.

- **Calculate your cash requirements**. What must you pay during this same period? This includes payroll, critical vendors, and any can't-miss obligations. For our example organization, this totaled $425,000.

- **Review your runway gap.** The difference between your liquidity and requirements reveals your runway gap. For our example organization, this was $65,000—the amount we needed to bridge to reach positive cash flow.

- **Assess your deferred obligations.** What payments have you already stretched beyond terms? Which vendors are already calling regularly? How much of this can you realistically negotiate? For our example organization, they had about

$290,000 in stretched obligations. We estimated we could negotiate extensions for $275,000 of this amount, leaving $15,000 that would need to be addressed immediately. This gave us a total runway need of $80,000 ($65,000 + $15,000). Adding a 25 percent contingency (because something always goes wrong), we arrived at a figure of $100,000. This was the amount we needed to secure for our recovery plan to succeed.

Working with leadership, we secured this runway through a combination of approaches: The founder borrowed $40,000 from a family member. We were more successful in negotiating with creditors than initially estimated. And most crucially, we received a large prepaid order from a client that provided essential liquidity. (Sometimes, it all comes down to a little bit of luck.)

That last point deserves emphasis: Fifteen years later, the company still gives that same client preferred pricing as a thank you. They have no idea that they literally saved the company.

This structured approach to runway assessment creates clarity that drives action. It transforms the overwhelming question of "How will we survive?" into a specific, quantifiable challenge: "How will we secure $100,000 in the next two weeks?"

The latter is answerable; the former just creates paralysis.

MESSY MOMENT: "SORRY, BROTHER" WAS ALL I COULD SAY

Sometimes, even correct decisions and actions turn out wrong. Prior to John and I combining forces, he was planning to buy a commercial property because a friend was giving him an unbelievable deal. He called me and wanted me to go in on it. Liz and I were living in Pennsylvania at the time. We decided to drive back to Ohio and see the property one of the following weekends.

The buildings were great, but the access to the property was brutal. The consulting firm I once worked for had an office in that area, so I called a partner from that office. He told me the original owners were clients. The property had been vacant for a long time, and he strongly advised me not to buy it. I called John and told him what I found out. I was too late—he had already bought it.

Fast-forward another year, when John and I decided to work together. The company was not in a good place, and he still had the property. It was sucking up resources we didn't have. I tried to find a solution, but nothing worked. Fortunately, John's extended family owned the largest auction company in Ohio. We decided to auction it. John connected with a friend to be at the auction to buy it, should the auction go horribly wrong. Two people showed for the auction, and one was our friend. Ouch.

Our friend didn't have to bid, and the property sold. John owed more than the purchase price, but I was able to work a deal with the lender. All good and behind us.

Fast-forward another few years, and natural gas was discovered in that part of Ohio. I drove past the property on a trip sometime later and saw the entire complex was full of natural gas trucks and equipment. I called John.

"Sorry, brother. You are not going to believe this, but looks like someone made a killing on your property."

Well. You can't win 'em all.

THE DON'T PERMIT LOSSES PRINCIPLE

One of the most critical principles I've applied across multiple turnarounds is what I call *Don't Permit Losses*. The concept is simple but powerful: Breaking even is actually losing.

Every day your business operates, it should generate profit. Not just revenue, not just growth, but actual profit. This might seem obvious, but I've encountered countless companies that operate for extended periods at or below breakeven, hoping that scale will eventually create profitability.

This hope is almost always misplaced. Businesses that can't generate profit at their current scale rarely find profitability by growing. Instead, unprofitable growth simply accelerates their path to failure.

For companies in crisis, enforcing profitability becomes even more critical. You simply don't have the luxury of running unprofitable operations while you figure things out. Every day must contribute to rebuilding your financial foundation, not eroding it further.

This principle guided our approach with another company facing crisis; rather than focusing exclusively on growth or cost-cutting, we redesigned their entire operation to ensure daily profitability. We eliminated service lines that couldn't generate consistent margins. We restructured contracts that didn't contribute to the bottom line. We prioritized profit over volume at every decision point.

The power of this principle is that it creates a virtuous cycle. Profitable days build cash reserves. Cash reserves create options. Options allow for strategic rather than reactive decisions. Strategic decisions improve profitability further. The company gets stronger with each passing day rather than weaker.

This focus on daily profitability doesn't mean ignoring long-term investments. It means being disciplined about which investments you make and ensuring they have a clear path to producing returns. For this organization, we continued investing in product development but with much more rigorous criteria for which features would actually drive revenue.

Handling unexpected expenses becomes much simpler when you're generating consistent profit. That's why liquidity matters—no liquidity means no options. When an unexpected cost arises in a profitable company with adequate reserves, it's an inconvenience rather than an existential threat.

The discipline of Don't Permit Losses is particularly important during recovery because it prevents backsliding. It's easy to rationalize "just this one" unprofitable decision or to temporarily return to old habits. But these exceptions quickly become the rule again, undermining your recovery momentum.

By enforcing profitability as a nonnegotiable principle— especially during recovery—you create the foundation for sustainable financial health.

CREATING FINANCIAL STRENGTH SYSTEMATICALLY

Building a balance sheet that can take a punch doesn't happen overnight. It requires systematic effort over time, following principles that might seem conservative during good periods but prove essential during challenges.

This systematic approach to financial strength is how I believe we created luck. When unexpected opportunities or challenges arose, we had the resources to respond effectively. We still had to be headed in the right direction, but we avoided fatal blows because our financial foundation was solid.

The reality is that nothing is linear in business recovery. Progress comes in fits and starts. You'll have unexpected setbacks alongside unexpected victories. The companies that survive and eventually thrive are those with financial systems that can absorb the inevitable volatility.

I witnessed this firsthand when I witnessed one company transform from financial distress to substantial financial resilience. Over two years, we systematically built cash reserves, reduced debt, and optimized their cost structure. This financial foundation enabled them to weather industry downturns that crushed competitors and ultimately positioned them for a successful exit that created significant wealth for all stakeholders.

Creating this systematic financial strength requires developing specific habits:

- **Establish clear financial thresholds.** What minimum cash reserve will you maintain? What debt-to-equity ratio will you target? What gross margins are best in class? These aren't abstract goals but firm guidelines that drive daily decisions.

- **Implement regular financial reviews that look beyond the P&L.** Weekly cash flow projections, monthly balance sheet analyses, and quarterly debt structure reviews keep financial health at the forefront of your planning.

- **Develop contingency plans before you need them**. What expenses could you cut if revenue dropped by 20 percent? What funding sources could you tap if an unexpected opportunity arose? Planning these responses in advance allows for faster, more effective action when challenges emerge.

- **Create a financial early warning system.** What metrics would indicate potential problems before they become crises? For different businesses, these might include changing sales cycles, increasing customer acquisition costs, or extending accounts receivable. Identifying these indicators early provides time to respond before a full-blown crisis develops.

- **Maintain the Founder's Math Hack as an ongoing discipline, not just a crisis tool.** Continuous clarity about your financial drivers creates better decisions in good times and bad.

These systematic approaches transformed the company we opened this chapter with from a company with thirty days of runway to one with six months of operating reserves. The same disciplines that enabled their recovery became the foundation for their sustained success.

Financial strength isn't just about avoiding failure—it's about creating options. Companies with strong balance sheets can pursue opportunities that others can't. They can invest when competitors are cutting back. They can focus on long-term value creation rather than short-term survival.

By building financial strength systematically, you're not just preparing for the next crisis—you're positioning your company for sustained success regardless of what the future holds.

MARCHING ORDERS

Now that you understand the components of both your Go-Forward Operating Plan and your Go-Forward Financial Plan, make sure to put the following strategies into action:

- Calculate your current runway using the framework provided: Timeline to positive cash flow, available liquidity, cash requirements, and deferred obligations.

- Identify your liquidity target using the six-month rule: Monthly fixed costs multiplied by six, or fixed costs minus agreement revenue multiplied by six.

- Add the top two to four financial priorities to your One Page Recovery Plan.

- Create your simplified financial dashboard focusing on your key economic drivers and the metrics that best reflect your specific business model.

- Develop your vendor communication plan for extended payment terms, acknowledging reality while providing a clear path to normalization.

- Apply the Founder's Math Hack to your specific situation, identifying the critical few variables that drive your financial performance.

- Implement the Don't Permit Losses principle immediately, evaluating every aspect of your business for profitability.

- Begin building systematic financial strength through clear thresholds, regular reviews, contingency planning, and early warning indicators.

NOTES FROM THE WAR ROOM

As you go about creating your Go-Forward Financial Plan, remember that liquidity gives you options, simplicity enables decision-making, and a strong balance sheet prepares you to take a punch. Creating systematic financial strength isn't just about survival; it's about positioning your company to seize opportunities that others can't.

One of the most important parts of any successful business, though? What really moves the needle when things get tough?

You guessed it: The people. In the next chapter, you'll learn how to build your Go-Forward Team.

CHAPTER 6

BUILD YOUR GO-FORWARD TEAM

BEING BOARD CHAIR OF A UNIVERSITY IN CRISIS IS NOT FOR THE faint of heart. Tough decisions need to be made quickly, which is especially challenging in higher education because nothing happens quickly. The board of trustees has several priorities in a shared-governance model, but the two most critical are being showcased in this book: (1) setting the direction of the university, and (2) who you select to lead the charge.

Remember the story of Malone doubling down on purpose in chapter 4? After we trustees unanimously agreed we were fully aligned with the Church, our next challenge was selecting our next president. We had to get this right.

Selecting our next president was an opportunity to send a clear signal to the market that we were serious about our new direction. It was about matching leadership to the challenge at hand. It was also about transitioning well because Malone had a history of poor leadership transition. The current president was retiring, and he and I (who are friends to this day) were committed to making the transition successful.

And because we were honest and clear, we did just that. We got it right. The new president (who is also a close friend) *is* the right person for the right moment. The results speak for themselves. For the first time in over ten years, Malone has experienced an increase in year-over-year undergrad FTE (full-time equivalent) enrollment. In an era when many similar institutions are closing their doors, Malone is on the rise.

I've seen this pattern play out over and over: Sometimes the most crucial decision during transformation isn't what to do, but who should lead the effort. Sometimes the right team—not just a new strategy—is the solution.

THE *WHO NOT HOW* PRINCIPLE IN ACTION

Nothing drove home the *Who Not How* principle (shout out to Dan Sullivan and Benjamin Hardy for that one[3]) more clearly than what happened at Gift·ology after John's passing. Continuing John's mission without his unique gifts seemed nearly impossible. He was our primary voice, our relationship builder, our greatest revenue generator. How could we possibly replace that?

The answer, of course, was that we couldn't—not directly. Instead, we had to build around the exceptional people we already had, particularly Mike Monroe.

Mike had been creating our content since the launch of Gift·ology. He understood John's mind better than anyone and could communicate what we stood for in a way nobody else could. He wasn't just a team member; he was a true partner in making Gift·ology happen.

This principle "who not how" completely flips how most leaders approach problems. Instead of asking, "How do we solve this problem?" the better question is, "Who can solve this problem?"

---

3   Dan Sullivan and Benjamin Hardy, *Who Not How: The Formula to Achieve Bigger Goals Through Accelerating Teamwork* (Hay House, Inc, 2020).

Here's what I've learned: The capacity of the right person far exceeds the capacity of even the best system or strategy. Systems and strategies matter, but they can't make up for having the wrong people in critical roles. Different phases of business require different leadership capabilities. The skills that launch a business aren't always the same ones that scale it. The leadership needed during stable periods might not be what's required during transformation. This isn't a failure of the individuals involved—it's simply matching the right capabilities to the current challenge.

At Gift·ology, after John's passing, Mike's leadership allowed us to accelerate initiatives like the R.I.C.H. Relationship Society and the completion of Beyond Gift·ology—projects that created pathways forward we couldn't have imagined otherwise.[4]

The beauty of focusing on "who" before "how" is that it acknowledges human potential as your greatest asset. When you find the right who, they'll often figure out the how.

ASSESSING YOUR CURRENT TEAM

When crisis hits, everyone wants to look outside for help—hire consultants, bring in new leadership, find different talent. I get it. But I've consistently found that most organizations already have the talent they need—they just haven't properly identified or positioned it.

Seeing your team clearly during crisis means looking beyond résumés or performance reviews. You need to watch for behaviors that often go unnoticed during normal times.

---

4   R.I.C.H. Relationships Society, Gift·ology, August 22, 2024, https:// Gift·ologygroup.com/rich-relationships/.

- **Who stays calm when everything's falling apart?** Crisis amplifies everything—especially emotions. The people who maintain their composure when chaos erupts are gold, regardless of their title or experience.

- **Who jumps to solutions instead of playing the blame game?** When things go wrong, some people instinctively look for who caused the problem. Others immediately start working on fixes. You want the fixers front and center during transformation.

- **Who keeps performing without being micromanaged?** During crisis, you can't hover over everyone. The people who maintain productivity with minimal guidance are the ones creating stability that allows you to focus on critical decisions.

- **Who tells it like it is?** Crisis requires honest communication. People who can deliver difficult messages clearly while still being empathetic are essential during turnarounds.

- **Who adapts quickly when circumstances change?** The ability to pivot as situations evolve makes all the difference. Look for people who can adjust without becoming defensive or resistant.

Here's what's fascinating: These capabilities often have nothing to do with titles or tenure. Sometimes your most effective crisis leaders are hiding in plain sight, doing jobs that don't fully tap their potential.

At Gift·ology, after John's passing, we discovered Sara Hardwick's untapped potential. Initially hired to help develop and run R.I.C.H., we realized she could take on a much broader role in promoting *Beyond Gift·ology* through podcasts and stages. Her ability to communicate our message with clarity and conviction was exactly what we needed during this critical transition.

To find these hidden stars, you need to have honest conversations throughout your organization. Ask team members who they go to when they need help solving problems. Watch who other people turn to during stressful situations. Notice whose judgment people trust when facing uncertainty.

This isn't about creating competition or undermining your formal leadership structure. It's about seeing the actual capabilities within your organization so you can align roles with abilities during transformation.

And remember—this assessment works both ways. Some highly effective team members during stable periods may struggle during crisis. This isn't a judgment of their value but a recognition that different circumstances call for different capabilities.

THE HIDDEN ASSETS ON YOUR TEAM

Some of your most valuable resources may be operating completely under the radar—people whose contributions are essential but largely invisible in your formal structure. Finding and leveraging these hidden assets can completely change the game during transformation.

I've seen this pattern in virtually every turnaround I've led. In one technology company, the wife of the CEO had been handling "miscellaneous administrative tasks" but actually possessed extraordinary organizational skills and a service delivery focus. When we recognized and formalized her role, operations improved dramatically, and service delivery performance shot up. This also allowed her husband to focus on sales and technical oversight. The combination was effective.

These hidden assets often come from surprising places. I've repeatedly found tremendous value in the spouses of the leadership team. In three separate turnarounds, spouses played critical roles in the transformation—not because of nepotism but because they brought valuable perspectives and exceptional talent. They often see the organization more objectively than those embedded in day-to-day operations.

Also, look at people who operate across different departments or regularly interact with external stakeholders. These folks often have unique visibility into organizational bottlenecks and customer needs. They may have developed informal solutions that could be formalized and scaled.

Don't overlook your part-time, contract, or consultant relationships either. Sometimes the person with the clearest perspective on your challenges isn't fully embedded in your organization. Their partial outsider status can provide valuable objectivity during crisis.

When identifying these hidden assets, forget about traditional credentials. The most valuable people during transformation may not have impressive degrees or extensive experience in their current role. Instead, they demonstrate practical problem-solving abilities, entrepreneurial thinking, and emotional resilience—qualities that don't always show up on résumés.

Once identified, integrating these hidden assets takes careful handling. You need to create appropriate roles that leverage their strengths without creating unnecessary disruption. Be transparent about why these changes are happening—it's about matching capabilities to current needs, not playing favorites.

In Gift·ology, after John's passing, we recognized that our Gift·ologist team had been working with John for years—they understood how to deliver excellence to our clients in a way no new hire could match. Similarly, our gifting specialist team had been fulfilling gifting deals effectively for a long time. We needed to build around these existing strengths rather than trying to reinvent our approach.

Sometimes this process means replacing several underperforming team members with fewer high performers who better match your current needs. I call this the "trade three for two" principle. This isn't just cost-cutting; it's about creating a more effective team structure built around your truly exceptional people.

By finding and properly positioning the hidden assets on your team, you create a more nimble, responsive organization capable of navigating transformation successfully.

MESSY MOMENT: PARTNER WELL

John was the perfect partner for me. He pitched me as being calm under pressure. I don't know if that is actually true, but I can say with certainty that all of us have tough moments.

One for me was several years ago. I'll spare you the backstory, but I found myself increasingly involved in a company we had partnered with. The company had a very high upside, undoubtedly the highest upside of any company we had partnered with at that point. However, for many reasons, there were also constant challenges.

Along the journey, I was asked by the board to increase my involvement. I reluctantly agreed in order to help protect the capital invested by many, including us. I also believed (and still do) that the solution fulfilled a large market need. The whole situation caused me a lot of stress. One Friday, I felt completely defeated. Money is always tight with high-growth companies, and we were facing an urgent capital need. The capital markets had really tightened up, so finding capital was becoming increasingly difficult. We had capital committed, but we needed to bridge a gap: Specifically, $500,000 by Monday. All our efforts throughout the week resulted in exactly zero dollars.

John knew it was a tough week, and like he often did, he FaceTimed me late that afternoon. I was tired, stressed, and completely overwhelmed. I could literally feel John's empathy through the video. He prayed for the situation and for me. With John, his concern was authentic and never surfaced. He cared so deeply that you knew he felt what you felt.

An hour later, I was getting ready to leave for a long, stressful weekend when I received a text message from our controller. She had just opened the mail and sent me a picture of a $500,000 check we received as part of COVID relief funds. The timing was surreal. God provided, and I called John back to experience that moment together.

MAKING THE DIFFICULT DECISIONS

No matter how carefully you assess your team and find hidden assets, transformations almost always require difficult personnel decisions. How you handle these moments affects not just the individuals involved—it shapes your entire culture and determines whether your remaining team will fully commit to the path forward.

I've learned the hard way that cutting once is always better than cutting twice. Making incremental reductions in hopes that things will improve rarely works and only prolongs organizational anxiety. It's far better to make a single, well-considered decision about your team structure than to create waves of uncertainty through multiple rounds of changes.

This requires brutal honesty in your assessment. If your financial model indicates you can only support $120,000 (or $1.2 million, doesn't matter) in monthly operating expenses, then you need to build a team within that constraint—not hope that growth will eventually solve the problem. Remember what I said earlier: Breaking even is actually losing when you're in recovery. You must design your team to generate profit from day one of your transformation.

When reductions are necessary, your approach makes all the difference. As a founder or leader, you can't delegate this responsibility, especially for team members who have shown commitment to your organization. They deserve to hear directly from you. If this happens, remember the following:

- **Focus on dignity rather than defensiveness**. The temptation is to justify your decision with elaborate explanations. Instead, be straightforward about the business reality while acknowledging the person's contributions. Make it clear that this is about organizational needs, not personal failings.

- **Be generous where possible**. If you can provide severance, extended benefits, or connections to new opportunities, do so. This isn't just kindness—it's pragmatic. How you treat departing team members sends a powerful message to those who remain.

- **Communicate the complete plan at once.** Don't drag out announcements over days or weeks. Once decisions are made, share the entire organizational change simultaneously so everyone understands the full picture.

- **Immediately reassure your key players**. Your A-team players will naturally wonder if they're next. Be explicit about their importance to the go-forward plan.

- **Adjust compensation along with team structure (in some cases)**. I've often found it effective to cut deeper in headcount but increase compensation for critical team members. This sends a clear message about who is essential to your future and ensures they don't start looking elsewhere during uncertainty.

The goal is to make these difficult decisions in a way that allows healing to begin immediately. The faster you can move through this phase, the sooner your team can focus fully on the path forward rather than worrying about what might happen next.

Remember that your remaining team is watching closely, not just listening to your words but observing how you treat people during difficult transitions. By handling these moments with clarity and compassion, you build the foundation for the engaged, committed team you'll need for successful transformation.

CRISIS COMMUNICATION THAT BUILDS CONFIDENCE

When your organization is in crisis, communication becomes both more difficult and more essential. Your team is hungry for clarity but often afraid of what they might hear. How you communicate during this period doesn't just share information—it either builds or erodes the confidence needed for successful transformation.

Your team already knows there's a problem. Pretending otherwise destroys credibility. When I met with our Gift·ology team after John's passing, I had to acknowledge that I didn't yet have all the answers. This honesty builds trust more effectively than false certainty.

Share what you know and admit what you don't. In those initial days after John's passing, I told our team: "This is going to be a process and it's going to take time. We are going to continue to teach the world to love like John loved. How that looks, I don't 100 percent know. Other than to say we will do it together."

Especially when times are tough, remember the following:

- **Give people something stable to hold onto.** In turbulence, people seek solid ground. Identify what isn't changing—your core values, commitment to clients, or long-term mission—to provide psychological anchors.

- **Be clear about immediate priorities**. Give specific direction about what needs to happen today and this week. Keep these directives simple and specific.

- **Don't make promises you can't keep about job security, financial recovery, or timelines.** These create expectations that, if unmet, will destroy trust when you need it most.

- **Looking backward to assign blame is a waste of precious energy.** Crisis response requires forward focus. Regardless of how you got here, energy spent on blame is energy diverted from solutions.

- **Avoid minimizing the situation.** Phrases like "this is just a bump in the road" or "we'll be fine" feel reassuring, but can backfire by suggesting you don't understand the situation's gravity.

- **Use action words.** When communicating difficult realities, always pair them with actionable next steps. This transforms potentially paralyzing information into motivation for focused effort.

By communicating effectively when your business is on the brink, you create the foundation of trust and shared understanding essential for transformation. People can endure tremendous challenges if they believe their leaders are being straight with them and have a credible path forward.

CREATING EARLY WINS THAT BUILD MOMENTUM

Transformation is a marathon, but people need sprint victories to stay engaged. Creating and celebrating early wins isn't just about morale—it's about proving that change is possible and building momentum toward larger goals.

When we launched Mission 600 after John's passing—our plan to secure six hundred memberships in our new community to replace lost revenue streams—we knew we needed incremental successes to demonstrate viability. Each new membership became a small victory we could celebrate, building confidence in our overall approach.

Early wins have to be genuine achievements, not manufactured successes. Your team can spot the difference between real progress and symbolic gestures.

They should connect directly to your core transformation goals, not peripheral activities. The win should demonstrate movement toward your ultimate objective.

Make sure they're visible and measurable. Vague improvements don't build momentum—clear, demonstrable progress does.

Try to involve multiple team members. Wins that engage only a small subset of your organization don't create the collective momentum you need.

Look for winnable battles that matter—meaningful but achievable objectives. This requires honest assessment of what's possible in your current state.

When selecting these early win opportunities, I look for efforts that have high probability of success, can be completed relatively quickly (thirty to sixty days), will produce visible results, require minimal additional resources, and engage key team members whose buy-in is essential.

How you communicate these wins matters tremendously. Celebrate them authentically but avoid overstatement. Acknowledge the win while connecting it to the larger transformation: "This is an important step that demonstrates we're on the right path."

Creating a regular cadence of these victories shifts organizational psychology from "Can we do this?" to "How quickly can we do this?" Each success builds credibility for your approach and generates energy for tackling larger challenges.

Pay special attention to wins that surprise skeptics. When someone who doubted your approach sees tangible results, their conversion becomes a powerful force for broader buy-in.

Early wins also provide opportunities to recognize team members, reinforcing behaviors essential for your transformation. This recognition doesn't require elaborate programs—sincere, specific acknowledgment of contributions does more than generic praise or token rewards.

Remember that early wins, while important, are not the finish line. They're mile markers that indicate you're moving in the right direction. Celebrate them briefly, learn from them consistently, and use them to build momentum toward your larger transformation goals.

MAINTAINING TEAM ALIGNMENT DURING CHANGE

Even with the right team in place and early wins building momentum, maintaining alignment during transformation doesn't happen by accident. Without some structure, even the most talented teams can fragment under pressure.

I've found that establishing a consistent meeting rhythm is absolutely essential. When we transformed Gift·ology after John's passing, we were already using the EOS model, which gave us a structured approach to keeping everyone focused on our priorities:

- These meetings aren't just about sharing information—they're about reinforcing direction and ensuring coordinated action. We use **daily standups** (not EOS but effective in crisis) lasting ten to fifteen minutes where team members share their top priorities and any obstacles they're facing. These brief check-ins prevent misalignment from persisting for more than twenty-four hours.

- We have **weekly tactical meetings** focused on addressing immediate issues, measuring progress against key metrics, and coordinating cross-functional activities. These meetings are highly structured with clear agendas and outcomes.

- We step back for **monthly strategic sessions** where we assess progress against our transformation plan, identify emerging challenges, and make adjustments as needed. These deeper dives prevent tactical focus from obscuring our strategic direction.

- We do **quarterly full-day reviews** that step all the way back to evaluate our overall approach, celebrate progress, and reset priorities for the coming quarter. These sessions reconnect our team to the bigger picture of transformation.

The structure of these meetings significantly impacts their effectiveness. Every meeting should have a clear purpose that participants understand in advance, defined roles, established ground rules, and measurable outcomes that will be evaluated at the next meeting.

Beyond formal meetings, maintaining alignment requires consistent one-on-one connections with key team members. These conversations provide space for concerns or ideas that might not surface in group settings and allow you to gauge how individuals are processing the transformation.

Tools like scorecards and dashboards create shared visibility into progress, making alignment less dependent on meetings. When everyone can see key metrics in real time, you reduce the "telephone game" effect of information passing through multiple people.

By ensuring everyone is moving in the same direction, you free mental energy that would otherwise be spent on coordination to focus instead on improvement and adaptation.

MARCHING ORDERS

Ready to shore up your Go-Forward Team? Take a deep breath, simplify, and focus. Here's what you need to do:

- Add the top two to four team priorities to your One Page Recovery Plan.

- Identify three potential hidden assets in your organization— people whose capabilities exceed their current role or whose contributions aren't fully recognized in your formal structure.

- Create your crisis communication plan that acknowledges reality while providing clear direction for immediate action.

- Establish your meeting rhythm for the recovery period, defining the frequency, purpose, and format for daily, weekly, monthly, and quarterly connections.

- Identify three potential early wins that are achievable within thirty to sixty days and will demonstrate meaningful progress toward your transformation goals.

- Develop a simple scorecard with three to five key metrics that will create visibility and alignment across your team during transformation.

- Have direct conversations with your A-players to reinforce their importance to your go-forward plan and address any concerns about stability.

NOTES FROM THE WAR ROOM

Nobody exemplified the power of focusing on people more than John, both as a businessman and as my dear friend. After his passing, I saw Mike Monroe step up to the plate in a tremendous way, taking some of the weight I was carrying off my shoulders with commendable solidarity and strength during one of the most challenging times of our lives.

The bottom line? Even the best financial and operating plans are secondary to the people next to you as you implement them. Crisis reveals who people really are—pay attention to who maintains composure, focuses on solutions, and inspires others when pressure is highest; these are your transformation leaders, regardless of title. Choose wisely.

In the next and final chapter, we'll look at how to bring it all together with—you guessed it—another plan, this time focused on execution.

CHAPTER 7

CREATE YOUR GO-FORWARD EXECUTION PLAN

NO MAJOR WEALTH-CREATING EVENT HAPPENS BY ACCIDENT. YOU may be thinking, *I'm a long way from a wealth-creating event.* Let me tell you a story: One of the companies we partnered with was in the chronic underperformance crisis, or the hamster wheel. When we first got involved, they were struggling to find direction and consistent performance. They had decent revenue but lacked focus, chasing opportunities across multiple industries with no clear strategy. Despite the founder's technical brilliance and twenty-year history, the business wasn't generating the returns it should have been.

We followed the playbook I lay out in *this* book, which resulted in dramatically improved earnings, target level liquidity gain, and a company ready to scale. This begs the question: Where should we focus our growth? The founder had a lot of medical clients and a desire to serve more. With this in mind, the answer emerged quickly: Focus on medical. While they had clients across various industries, focusing on healthcare allowed us to focus our resources, including marketing and service delivery and team composition, on serving this sector. The byproduct was that we were shaping the company into something a specific type of buyer would find irresistible.

It worked.

Less than three years after implementing this strategy, the company was acquired by a larger, equity-backed MSP that was focused on healthcare. The founders realized a multi-million dollar exit that far exceeded what would have been possible without this deliberate approach.

This wasn't just luck. The same pattern played out over and over. My point is simple: Strategy plus good execution wins big. You need both. That's why it's essential to remain focused on the macro—the direction—while ensuring excellent execution through systematic approaches. This final piece—how you execute day to day—makes the difference between a good idea and a successful transformation.

HOW THE THREE PLANS WORK TOGETHER HOLISTICALLY

Throughout this book, we've talked about three essential plans for your One Page Recovery Plan: your Go-Forward Operating Plan, your Go-Forward Financial Plan, and your Go-Forward Team Plan. I separated them to make things clearer, but in real life, they're completely intertwined.

Think of it this way: Your Go-Forward Operating Plan is the "what" and "why" of your business. It clarifies your purpose and focuses your activities on the few critical priorities using your key economic drivers that will drive transformation. But without money and people, it's just a nice document collecting dust on your shelf.

Your Go-Forward Financial Plan ensures you've got the resources to make your Go-Forward Operating Plan happen. It establishes liquidity (remember: take a punch) and creates the runway you need for real progress. But financial discipline alone doesn't create results.

Your Go-Forward Team Plan is what turns ideas and resources into reality. It ensures you have the right people in the right roles doing the right things. Without this human element, your operating and financial plans remain theoretical exercises.

The key is understanding how these plans interact. Your financial constraints directly impact what's possible in your operating plan because your monthly expenses create clear boundaries for what you can do and who you can have on your team.

Similarly, your team capabilities influence your operating priorities. At Gift·ology, after John's passing, we built our operating plan around growing the R.I.C.H. Relationship Society using Mike Monroe's unique ability to articulate our message because that was our strongest asset. The strategy followed the talent, not the other way around.

When these plans work together harmoniously, they create a virtuous cycle. Your operating clarity enables better financial decisions. Your financial discipline creates stability that attracts and retains talent. Your team capabilities open new strategic possibilities that improve financial performance.

This integration doesn't happen by itself. You have to deliberately connect the dots. Review all three dimensions together regularly. Ask yourself: Are our operating priorities still aligned with our financial realities? Does our team have what it needs to execute our plan? Do our financial metrics reflect our strategic priorities?

By keeping this holistic perspective, you avoid the common trap of over-focusing on one dimension while neglecting others. Recovery requires all three elements working together, reinforcing rather than undermining each other.

FROM RECOVERY TO SUSTAINABLE GROWTH

There's a moment in every successful turnaround when you move from fighting for survival to building for the future. This transition is both exciting and dangerous; I've seen organizations nail it perfectly and others stumble just when success seemed assured. The tendency is to exhale and allow a "Boy, I'm glad that's over" mindset to seep in.

How do you know when you've reached this turning point? I look for several indicators: You've been consistently profitable for at least six months. Your operating metrics show stability rather than volatility. Your team is proposing improvements instead of just following directions. Your customers are sticking around and even referring others. And most importantly, you've built enough financial cushion to absorb normal business fluctuations without panicking.

When these conditions are present, it's time to shift your approach—not throwing out the disciplines that got you here, but adapting them for growth.

The company with the major wealth-creating event (not surprisingly) made this transition beautifully. After stabilizing the business and establishing a clear healthcare focus, we gradually expanded our service offerings within that vertical. We invested in advanced security capabilities that our medical clients increasingly demanded. We developed specialized compliance expertise that differentiated us from competitors. Each expansion built on our core strengths while extending our value proposition.

The key was maintaining our strategic clarity even as our tactical options multiplied. We didn't chase every opportunity that emerged—we evaluated each against our long-term vision of being the premium healthcare MSP in our region.

This disciplined expansion accelerated our growth while actually improving our margins, setting the stage for the eventual acquisition. We were no longer just surviving; we were systematically building value.

At the same time, you can't abandon the financial disciplines established during recovery. Growth can consume cash even faster than crisis if not managed carefully. The liquidity you've built provides options, but preserving financial strength remains essential.

The organizations that navigate this transition most successfully maintain what Jim Collins calls "productive paranoia." They don't forget the lessons of crisis even as conditions improve. They build early warning systems to detect problems before they become crises. They maintain contingency plans that can be activated quickly if needed.

This balanced approach—maintaining core disciplines while adapting for growth—creates the foundation for sustainable success rather than a temporary recovery followed by renewed crisis.

MESSY MOMENT: LEARN TO CELEBRATE

My biggest regret since John passed away is that we never truly celebrated our wins. I assume it is common for people wired like us to quickly focus on the next thing. This same trait is likely true of many people reading this book. John and I were grinding for years because there was always the next goal, the next key strategy to accomplish, the next target to hit.

Also, if we are being honest, I don't think we ever celebrated because we never felt like we were worth celebrating. I have spent many hours since John passed away thinking about our eighteen years together as partners. I find it interesting that no matter how many wins one accumulates, you never quite feel like you're as good as others perceive you to be. Deep down, John and I were two kids from farm country Ohio, trying to figure out how we got here.

Our friends Hal Elrod and Cameron Herold tell entrepreneurs in their book *The Miracle Morning for Entrepreneurs*: "It is vitally important that you give yourself permission to feel proud of yourself." I cannot recall one conversation John and I had over eighteen years of being proud of what we built. That's sad. I am incredibly proud of John. I knew him before he was John Ruhlin on stage and in lights, and he was the same guy.

I'm humbled that we strived every day to live in obedience to what we felt we were called to do. I am praying for you as you use this book as a guide through a challenge. I'm also praying that you learn to celebrate along the way.

IMPLEMENTING EOS AS YOUR OPERATING SYSTEM

Through all my years turning companies around, I've learned that even the best strategy fails without systematic execution. You need an operating system that turns your high-level plans into daily actions and creates accountability at every level.

After trying various approaches, I've found that the EOS model developed by Gino Wickman provides the most effective framework for post-crisis execution.[5] In fact, as I mentioned, we implement EOS in every company we partner with—it's that fundamental to sustainable success.

---

5   Gino Wickman, *Traction: Get A Grip on Your Business* (BenBella Books, 2013).

Why EOS? Simple: Before implementation, you may have good people and good services but lack the organizational discipline to execute consistently. Decisions may sit in limbo without clear ownership. Priorities can shift weekly, creating confusion and wasted effort. Meetings can be mostly status updates rather than solving problems.

After implementing EOS, organizations gain both clarity and momentum. The team understands the company's priorities and their specific roles in achieving them. Meetings become focused and productive. Issues are identified and addressed systematically rather than lingering unresolved.

One of the most powerful elements of EOS is the accountability chart, which differs significantly from a traditional org chart. Instead of just showing reporting relationships, it clarifies who owns what functions and outcomes. This eliminates the confusion and finger-pointing that often plague struggling organizations.

Another crucial aspect is the establishment of rocks—clear, specific priorities for each quarter that advance your annual and long-term objectives. These aren't vague aspirations but concrete deliverables with defined owners and timelines. By limiting the number of rocks each quarter (typically three to five for the company and one to three per person), you create the focus essential for consistent progress.

The weekly meeting rhythm in EOS creates the consistent check-ins needed to maintain momentum without micromanagement. These aren't tedious status meetings but structured sessions that identify and solve problems while reinforcing priorities and accountability.

What makes EOS particularly effective for post-crisis organizations is that it scales with you. The same principles work whether you have ten employees or a hundred. The framework grows with your organization while maintaining consistent execution discipline.

While I specifically recommend EOS, the core principles apply regardless of what system you choose: Clear ownership of responsibilities, limited and specific priorities, consistent meeting rhythms, and measurable outcomes. The key is having some systematic approach rather than relying on heroic individual efforts or management by crisis.

Remember that implementing any operating system requires patience and persistence. You won't achieve perfect execution immediately. What matters is establishing the framework and then improving incrementally over time. Eventually, the discipline of the process becomes part of your organizational DNA, creating sustainable execution excellence.

BUILDING ORGANIZATIONAL HABITS THAT LAST

Transforming an organization isn't a one-time event—it's about establishing new patterns that stick long after the initial crisis has passed. In my experience, sustainable transformation depends less on grand strategies and more on the daily habits that drive consistent execution.

Systems outlast motivation every time. When motivation wanes—as it inevitably does—systems keep you moving forward. This is why building durable organizational habits is essential for long-term success.

The most important habits center around how you use time. At Gift·ology, even after John's passing, we maintained the meeting rhythm we had established years earlier. This wasn't just about sharing information; it was about reinforcing priorities, catching issues early, and maintaining collective focus.

Our weekly meetings have a consistent structure: We start with good news, review scorecard metrics, discuss progress on rocks, identify and solve issues, and recap to-dos. This routine creates a heartbeat for the organization that continues regardless of what's happening externally.

Beyond meetings, we've built habits around how we capture and use information. Every client interaction gets documented in our CRM. Every project follows standardized workflows. Every financial decision is evaluated against our established criteria. These aren't exciting practices, but they create the consistency that enables excellence.

Documentation is another critical habit that prevents backsliding. When we identify a successful approach, we document it immediately, creating standard operating procedures that preserve institutional knowledge. This prevents the common cycle of solving the same problems repeatedly because solutions weren't properly captured.

I recommend connecting these habits to your organization's purpose and values. When people understand why a particular practice matters—how it contributes to your larger mission—they're more likely to maintain it even when immediate pressures don't demand it. At Gift·ology, for example, our documentation habits are tied directly to our commitment to excellent client experiences. Our clients are trusting us with their most important relationships. We take this very seriously because we know this list is currency for our clients. Everyone understands that capturing information isn't just administrative busywork; it's essential to delivering the personalized service our clients expect.

The organizations that sustain transformation over the long term are those that embed their new approaches into daily routines. When excellence becomes habitual rather than exceptional, you've truly transformed your organization beyond just surviving the immediate crisis.

MAINTAINING DISCIPLINE THROUGH CHANGE

One of the greatest challenges in sustained transformation is fighting the inevitable "crisis fatigue" that emerges over time. The adrenaline and focus that carried your team through initial crisis phases naturally diminishes. As conditions improve, the urgency that drove difficult decisions and extraordinary effort begins to fade.

This transition period is where many transformations falter. People start slipping back into old habits. Exceptions to new protocols begin to multiply. The discipline that enabled recovery begins to erode, often so gradually that it's not immediately apparent.

I've seen this pattern repeatedly, and it's why I'm obsessive about maintaining discipline even as circumstances change. At the company with the major wealth-creating event, we were relentless about reinforcing our core disciplines even as the business stabilized and began to grow. We didn't relax our standards just because the immediate crisis had passed.

To maintain discipline through these transitional periods, try the following:

- **Keep your scorecard metrics visible to everyone, updated consistently, and referenced in every major meeting.** When performance starts to slip, it's immediately apparent rather than hidden until it becomes problematic.

- **Don't start canceling or rescheduling your established meetings**. The moment you do, you signal that discipline is optional rather than essential.

- **Celebrate when people follow the process, not just when they get good results.** Recognize team members who maintain discipline even when immediate results don't demand it. This reinforces that how you work matters as much as what you achieve.

- **Be incredibly careful about making exceptions.** The moment you start making exceptions to your established processes, you create precedents that undermine the entire system. If adjustment is truly needed, change the process officially rather than simply bypassing it.

- **When you see team members reverting to old patterns, address it quickly and specifically.** Letting these moments pass sends a powerful message that discipline isn't actually required.

Maintaining discipline doesn't mean becoming rigid. Your processes and priorities will evolve as circumstances change. The key is making these changes deliberately and systematically rather than through neglect or exception.

This balance—maintaining core disciplines while adapting to changing conditions—is perhaps the greatest test of leadership during transformation. Those who navigate it successfully create organizations that don't just survive crisis but become more resilient and capable with each challenge they face.

ADAPTING YOUR PLAN AS CONDITIONS CHANGE

No plan survives contact with reality unchanged. The assumptions underlying your initial recovery approach will inevitably prove incomplete or incorrect as circumstances evolve. Your ability to adapt—without losing focus or abandoning core principles—determines whether transformation continues or stalls. We have made countless changes to Mission 600, including the question of how we can make it Mission 300.

There's a crucial distinction between pivoting and wandering: Pivoting means making deliberate adjustments based on new information while maintaining your fundamental direction, and wandering means reacting to each new development without strategic coherence.

At a technology firm in crisis, we initially focused on stabilizing using the plans from this book. Once we were stable, we needed to focus on growth. We were a cloud provider for a long-term care application, and we needed to not only build a new cloud environment but also relocate it to a new data center built twenty minutes down the road. Factoring in the license cost savings, we made the decision to utilize Microsoft's hypervisor versus the more dominant VM Ware solution. While our tech team was more familiar with VM Ware, they wanted a new environment, and using Microsoft made more economic sense which made the funding possible. This pivot of investing in the Microsoft technology stack positioned us perfectly for a later acquisition by a larger firm looking to expand and specifically seeking Microsoft expertise. Were we lucky? Yes. But had we not been adaptable this outcome would have been more difficult to achieve and may not have materialized.

That begs the question: How do you know when adjustment is necessary?

- **Watch for consistent underperformance against key metrics despite faithful execution of your plan.** If you're doing what you planned but not getting expected results, your assumptions need examination.

- **Pay attention to significant market or competitive changes that weren't anticipated in your original planning.** These may create either threats to your current approach or opportunities for acceleration.

- **Listen carefully to team feedback indicating consistent obstacles or inefficiencies in executing your plan.** This often reveals adjustment opportunities that aren't visible from leadership perspectives alone. When these signals appear, resist the urge to make immediate, reactive changes. Instead, verify the signal represents a genuine pattern rather than normal variation or temporary circumstances. A single week of missed metrics doesn't necessarily indicate a failing strategy.

- **Identify specifically what's not working as expected and why.** Is the issue with the strategy itself, execution approach, resource allocation, or external factors beyond your control?

- **Evaluate potential adjustments against your core recovery principles.** Will the change maintain focus on your key drivers? Is it consistent with your financial constraints? Does it leverage your team's actual capabilities? Then implement the adjustment decisively but with appropriate monitoring to ensure it delivers the intended improvement.

The most successful transformations I've led have required significant adaptation from initial plans, but these changes maintained consistent alignment with our fundamental direction and principles.

At Gift·ology after John's passing, our Mission 600 plan evolved substantially as we gained experience with our new community model and learned from others. We adjusted pricing structure, content delivery approach, and engagement strategies based on member feedback and performance data. These changes enhanced our effectiveness while maintaining our core focus on building a sustainable membership community.

The ability to adapt without losing momentum requires strong fundamentals—particularly the measurement systems and meeting rhythms we've discussed. When you have clear visibility into performance and regular forums to evaluate and adjust, you can evolve your approach without the disorientation that often accompanies significant changes.

Remember that adaptation isn't failure—it's learning. The most dangerous mindset during transformation is clinging to the original plan despite evidence it needs refinement. Your initial approach was based on limited information; as you generate new data through execution, incorporating these insights only strengthens your path forward.

MESSY MOMENT: WIDE AWAKE

Three a.m. I don't know what it is about three a.m., but I frequently wake up and can't sleep. Does that happen to you? Even now, after all these years of being in messy situations, I still wake up with my mind racing. Nothing is linear is a phrase you will learn about in this book. It refers to the truth that things will rarely play out exactly how you planned them. I know this because I have experienced it for over twenty years. Knowing this fact doesn't stop your mind from racing when reality happens. This is when I lean on the clear mind and calm spirit prayer mentioned in this book. I have learned that wisdom is often displayed when my mind is clear and my spirit is calm.

If you are awake at three a.m. today or tomorrow, I may be too. If I am, I will be praying the Lord grants you a clear mind and a calm spirit. I would appreciate your prayer for the same in return. Sleep tight!

MARCHING ORDERS

Ready, Set, Execute!

Remember:

- Implement a consistent meeting rhythm that includes daily check-ins, weekly tactical discussions, monthly strategic reviews, and quarterly planning sessions.

- Pinpoint five to seven metrics that include both leading and lagging indicators relevant to your specific transformation.

- Identify the three organizational habits most critical to maintaining your transformation momentum and develop specific plans to reinforce them.

- Develop your crisis fatigue mitigation strategy, focusing on how you'll maintain discipline as immediate pressures ease.

- Establish your celebration protocol to acknowledge milestones and reinforce progress without losing momentum.

NOTES FROM THE WAR ROOM

Execution determines whether your plans become reality; even the most brilliant strategy fails without systematic implementation. Remember that systems drive behavior more effectively than willpower, and our goal is to build organizational habits that maintain discipline even when motivation naturally fluctuates.

Because—and I hate to say it, but it's true—it's not a matter of when your business might face another crisis, it's when. The cycle goes round and round, and we get a little stronger each time.

CONCLUSION

NOW GO WIN

Seven months after John's passing, I stood on stage at our *Beyond Gift·ology* book launch. The room was packed with people who loved John—some who knew him personally, others who only knew him through his work. As I looked out at that crowd, I felt both the weight of responsibility and the surge of possibility.

After John died, we faced a critical decision at Gift·ology: Preserve what was or build what could be. We could have played it safe, trying to maintain what John had created, gradually diminishing over time. Instead, we chose transformation. We embraced the brutal fact that without John's unique gifts, we needed to become something different—not lesser, just different.

Our Mission 600 approach wasn't just theory or something I made up for this book. It was our actual plan for moving forward, built on the principles I've shared with you. We focused on what we still had rather than what we'd lost. We simplified our approach. We built around the strengths of our team, particularly Mike Monroe's extraordinary ability to capture John's voice and vision. We created a financial model that wasn't dependent on John's speaking revenue.

The results so far have been amazing. Our R.I.C.H. Relationship Society is growing steadily. *Beyond Gift·ology* is reaching people John never had the chance to connect with.

Most importantly, we're honoring John not by freezing his legacy in time but by allowing it to evolve through the people he touched.

I'm not sharing this to brag. In fact, our journey is still unfolding. But I *am* sharing to show you living proof that the principles in this book actually work. They're not theoretical concepts developed in a classroom. They're battle-tested approaches from ten real transformations, including our current journey at Gift·ology.

Whatever crisis you're facing right now—whether it's losing a key leader, slow erosion that's finally reached a breaking point, leadership challenges that require honest evaluation, or chronic underperformance that's keeping you from your potential—the path forward follows the same fundamental principles.

MESSY MOMENT: FINISH WELL

I know the feeling of facing pending failure. You want to be confident, but the surmounting list of company-ending possibilities quickly overcast the narrow path to victory. I cannot guarantee success, but I can say your best path forward is to focus your energy, effort, and prayers on the narrow path. I have found that focusing on the narrow path over a small amount of time miraculously makes the narrow path appear wider and the surmounting list of company-ending possibilities less intimidating. I know this book can guide you to develop the path forward. Only you can determine the outcome. I'll leave you with this: The score at halftime doesn't matter so win the second half.

I'll be cheering you on.

TURN CRISIS INTO OPPORTUNITY

Throughout this book, I've emphasized something I've seen over and over: Crisis creates possibilities that comfort never could. When things are working "well enough," there's little reason to question fundamental assumptions or try radically different approaches. Crisis strips away that complacency.

The pivot that led to Gift·ology's success and the creation of Ruhlin Partners would never have happened without the financial pressure that forced John and me to rethink our business model. The Ruhlin Way would never have been created without the conflicts that threatened our partnership. Our most important innovations came not from comfort but from necessity.

This pattern holds true everywhere I look. The companies that emerge strongest from crisis are those that use it as an opportunity to challenge assumptions, refocus on fundamentals, and reimagine possibilities. They don't just survive crisis; they transform through it.

The question isn't whether you'll face crisis; you will. The question is whether you'll merely endure it or use it as a catalyst for transformation. The choice is yours, and it begins with your mindset. See crisis not just as a problem to solve but as an opportunity to remake your organization in ways that weren't possible before.

THE THREE NONNEGOTIABLE PRINCIPLES

Through all the turnarounds I've led, three core principles have proven essential. They're not complicated, but they're nonnegotiable. If you get these right, you can overcome almost any challenge. If you miss any of them, recovery becomes exponentially harder.

- **Simplify how you view your organization.** Complexity is the enemy of execution, especially during crisis. When everything seems to be falling apart, the natural tendency is to try to fix every problem simultaneously. This approach almost always fails.

- **Know who you are personally and organizationally.** Crisis often tempts leaders to become someone they're not—to adopt personas or approaches that feel "strong" but aren't authentic. Similarly, organizations often try to become something they aren't rather than building on their actual strengths. Effective transformation starts with an honest assessment of who you are. What are your true capabilities as a leader? Where do you need support? What values will you not compromise regardless of pressure? For your organization, what are your genuine strengths? What is your authentic purpose? Who do you actually serve best?

- **Make a plan, make decisions, and move forward fast.** Knowledge without action is useless during crisis. Once you've simplified your view and clarified who you are, you must move decisively. Create your One Page Recovery Plan. Make the difficult decisions it requires. Begin execution immediately. I've seen too many leaders get stuck analyzing everything to death while conditions keep getting worse. Others make plans but delay implementing the tough parts, hoping things will magically improve on their own. Others move fast with no actual plan, acting on the "I have to do something mentality." However, directionless action isn't progress, and all of these approaches usually end in failure. The organizations that successfully transform through crisis are those that move quickly from understanding to action. They make decisions with the information available, knowing they'll need to adjust along the way but recognizing that delay is often more damaging than imperfection.

THE VALUE OF FAITH IN TRANSFORMATION

I've focused mostly on practical approaches throughout this book, but I'd be missing something important if I didn't share the faith perspective that has guided my own journey. You don't need to share my specific beliefs to benefit from these principles, but there's wisdom here that goes beyond particular traditions.

I often think about the story of Peter walking on water in Matthew 14. When he focused on Jesus, he accomplished the impossible. When he focused on the waves—the crisis surrounding him—he began to sink. Similarly, for me, when I pray for clarity in my thinking, I need to act on that clarity in obedience versus focusing on the waves of crisis around me. This shows something fundamental about transformation: What we focus on largely determines our outcomes.

During crisis, it's natural to become fixated on problems, threats, and limitations. These are real and must be acknowledged. But if they become your primary focus, they will consume all your attention and energy. By deliberately shifting focus to possibilities, strengths, and purpose, you create space for transformation to emerge.

I've also found that obedience is most tested during difficulty. I can't claim to understand the theology, but I have witnessed many miraculous events—each time, as a result of me acting boldly in obedience to what I felt called to do. Why ask for wisdom or a clear mind if you don't act on what you receive?

When things are going well, it's relatively easy to follow principles and maintain discipline. When crisis hits, the temptation to abandon these for quick fixes becomes much stronger. Yet it's precisely during these moments that sticking to core principles matters most.

In every turnaround I've led, there have been moments when short-term pressures pushed toward decisions that would compromise long-term viability. The discipline to maintain focus on sustainable solutions rather than quick fixes comes partly from experience but also from a deeper commitment to doing what's right rather than what's easy.

Crisis also reveals what we truly believe about leadership. Do we believe leadership is ultimately about control or about service? Do we see our role as protecting our own interests or as creating conditions where others can succeed? Do we build organizations primarily for our benefit or as vehicles for broader impact?

My partnership with John was built on shared values that went beyond business success. We believed we serve God through our companies and we should create value not just for ourselves but for our clients, our team members, and our communities. This purpose guided us through difficult decisions and sustained us through challenging periods.

I believe that challenges often prepare us for greater opportunities than we could imagine. Just as physical training builds capacity for more demanding activities, navigating crisis develops capabilities that enable larger impact. What seems like unbearable pressure in the moment often turns out to be preparation for an expanded purpose.

Our goal in transformation isn't just to survive crisis or even to build successful businesses. It's to become better stewards of the resources and opportunities entrusted to us. Be rich and be generous—this guided John and me, and it provides context for all the practical approaches I've shared with you.

That is guidance you're going to need, I have to say, because while I hope this book helps you navigate your current situation successfully, I'd be lying if I didn't acknowledge an uncomfortable truth: This won't be your last crisis. No matter how effectively you transform through your current challenges, future difficulties will eventually emerge.

This reality isn't pessimistic; it's pragmatic. Markets evolve, disrupting established business models. Technologies change, rendering previous capabilities obsolete. Competitors emerge from unexpected directions. Economic cycles turn. Black swan events happen. The list goes on and on.

By applying the principles in this book not just to your current situation but as ongoing practices, you create an organization that takes body blows without faltering and emerges from challenges stronger than before. That capability becomes perhaps your greatest strategic asset in an increasingly volatile business environment.

THE NEXT STEP

If you've read this far, you're clearly committed to transformation rather than just getting by. The question now isn't whether these principles can work—they've been proven across multiple industries and situations. The question is how you'll apply them to your specific circumstances, and your immediate next steps depend on where you are in your journey.

If you're in the midst of active crisis—facing imminent cash shortfall, major leadership transition, or severe performance challenges (the Fire or the Broken Mirror)—start here:

- Develop your One Page Recovery Plan using the template provided, making sure it covers all three dimensions: Operating, financial, and team.

- Establish your seventy-two-hour priorities and communicate them clearly to key stakeholders.

- Implement your measurement system to create visibility into performance against critical metrics.

- Begin your regular meeting rhythm to maintain focus and alignment throughout the transformation process.

If you're addressing slower erosion or chronic underperformance (the Slow Leak or the Hamster Wheel) rather than immediate crisis, your approach may be less urgent but should follow the same fundamental principles:

- Develop your Go-Forward Operating Plan focused on your core purpose and key economic drivers.

- Build your Go-Forward Financial Plan that establishes adequate liquidity while focusing on sustainable profitability.

- Structure your Go-Forward Team Plan to ensure you have the right capabilities in the right roles.

- Implement your execution system with clear metrics, consistent meeting rhythms, and defined accountability.

Regardless of your specific situation, remember that transformation isn't an event but a process. The initial actions establish direction, but sustained effort creates lasting change. Commit to the disciplines outlined in this book, not just for weeks or months but as fundamental approaches that will serve your organization for years to come.

Also, recognize that you don't have to navigate this journey alone. Seek wisdom from those who have traveled similar paths. Build a support network that provides both practical guidance and emotional reinforcement. Consider whether you need a guide who can provide external perspective and specialized expertise for your particular challenges.

Most importantly, maintain the balance of brutal honesty about current reality with grounded optimism about future possibilities. This tension—acknowledging difficulties while believing in your ability to overcome them—creates the foundation for effective transformation.

You have everything you need to begin this journey right now. The principles are clear. The tools are provided. The path has been walked by others who have successfully transformed through challenges similar to yours.

And now?

Go out there and win.

Not just survive, but *win*.

The difficulties you're facing aren't the end of your story; they're the foundation for your next chapter.

John believed that relationships take you places marketing can't. I believe that transformation takes you places that mere survival can't. By applying the principles in this book consistently and courageously, you can turn your current challenges into the catalyst for something far better than what existed before. For more support and resources, visit *businessonthebrink.com*.

The journey won't be easy, but it will be worth it. I've seen it happen time and again—organizations that seemed destined for failure transformed into something remarkable. Yours can be one of those stories. In fact, I believe it will be.

Don't fear the mess. Transform through it.

THE COMPLETE GIFT·OLOGY RECOVERY PLAN

OPENING CONTEXT: A REAL-TIME CASE STUDY

What follows isn't theoretical—it's the actual plan we're implementing at Gift·ology following John Ruhlin's passing. I've included it not as a template to copy, but as a concrete example of how the principles in this book look when applied to a specific situation. Study it for the thinking process rather than the specific solutions.

BRUTAL FACTS OF REALITY ASSESSMENT
Initial Crisis Evaluation

The unexpected loss of John, our primary spokesperson. John on stage being our highest performing lead generation effort.

- 70 percent of profitability tied to John's speaking and consulting

- Need for leadership transition during emotional upheaval

- Market perception challenges and stakeholder confidence

- Team morale and direction during transition

Opportunities

- Two years prior, John wanted to speak less to spend more time with his family so organizationally we were already shifting to support this goal.

- Fortunately, this effort resulted in key programs already being developed and key hires already in place, including the following:

  - Referral Partner Transformation Course.
  - R.I.C.H. Relationship Society (in beta).

- ◦ Sara Hardwick was hired to develop and run R.I.C.H. She was also positioned as a secondary option for stages.
- ◦ Brian McRae was a partner in the creation and delivery of R.I.C.H.

- Mike Monroe has been creating our content since the launch of Gift·ology. He understands John's mind better than anyone and is able to effectively communicate the ethos of Gift·ology.

- Our second book *Beyond Gift·ology* was already approved for writing.

- Our Gift·ologist team, led by Kami and Carissa, has been working with John for years, so they know how to deliver excellence to our clients.

- Our gifting specialist team has been fulfilling gifting deals for years.

- We have a large network of A-listers that want to help us continue John's legacy and support his family by helping Gift·ology thrive.

- I have followed my own rules, so I'm financially able to live on less income during our transition.

GIFT·OLOGY ONE PAGE RECOVERY PLAN
Clear Purpose Statement
We help leaders love on their relationships because everything rises and falls on relationships. Why? Because relationships take you places marketing can't.

GO-FORWARD OPERATING PLAN—MISSION 600

- Current state of Gift·ology is a gifting company that sells education. Our leads are generated by John on stage or podcast.

    - Our economic drivers based on profitability:
        - Keynote Presentations
        - Consulting Services
        - Done for You Gifting Services

- Future state of Gift·ology is an education company that sells gifting. Leads are generated, and our highest profit margin offerings will be independent of John.

    - Our future economic drivers based on profitability:
        - Referral Partner Transformation Course
        - R.I.C.H. Membership
        - Consulting Services
        - Done for You Gifting Services

- Mission 600. Reach six hundred R.I.C.H. memberships to replace lost revenue.

- Accelerate the official launch of R.I.C.H. Relationship Society

- Accelerate the completion and launch of *Beyond Gift·ology: Earn Endless Word-of-Mouth with a System That Turns Relationships into Referral Partners.*

GO-FORWARD FINANCIAL PLAN

- Rod and Lindsay will unencumber the company from their compensation by supporting our families outside Gift·ology for at least two years.

- Gift·ology must remain profitable as we pivot.

- Eliminate or suspend all fixed costs that do not directly support our key economic drivers.

GO-FORWARD TEAM PLAN

- Mike to become more active in growing Gift·ology services including completion of *Beyond Gift·ology*, growing R.I.C.H. Relationship Society, and inserting the *Beyond Gift·ology* referral system into our sales process.

- Align our teams with our gift agency services and our R.I.C.H. education programs.

- Sara to lead the promotion efforts of *Beyond Gift·ology* via podcasts and stages.

- The Gift·ologist team, led by Kami and Carissa, to drive new gifting business through referral relationships.

GIFT·OLOGY GO-FORWARD EXECUTION PLAN

We were already using Traction as a model so our team was able to create the following plans from our recovery plan.

- Three-Year Plan

   ◦ One-thousand-plus R.I.C.H. members.
   ◦ Gifting sales exceed current levels.
   ◦ We are organizationally nimble, with minimal capital requirements, and enormously profitable.
   ◦ Our marketing efforts are generating consistent leads, and our community is creating consistent referrals.

- We have best-in-class retention of members.
- Gift·ology team members are sought-after speakers and workshop trainers.
- Agency gifting sales are generating target product and consulting sales.
- R.I.C.H. and Agency sales processes are aligned.
- We have a clear road map to expand Gift·ology brand to one million followers.

- One-Year Plan

  - Three hundred-plus R.I.C.H. Members.
  - We will identify our most successful and cost-effective marketing channels and generate one thousand quality leads to support R.I.C.H. sales.
  - We will review and refine our brand messaging to ensure it is clear and aligns with our service offerings, and implement it across all customer-facing channels.
  - Gift·ologists will achieve a minimum of twenty-five new client onboards utilizing Referral Partner Transformation system to generate their own leads.
  - We will successfully land ten target stages and two podcasts per month.
  - *Beyond Gift·ology* will achieve at least two hundred reviews on Amazon.
  - We will document and communicate all core R.I.C.H. operational processes, ensuring they are clear and accessible to both staff and members.

TOOLS FOR TRANSFORMATION

OPENING CONTEXT: THE TOOLS

The Founder's Math Hack simplifies the financial levers that matter most, helping leaders quickly see where to focus for maximum return. Once that clarity is established, the Debt Matrix provides a framework to reduce pressure on cash flow and free up capital through smart debt prioritization. Finally, the Runway Calculator turns your operating plan into a clear timeframe, showing exactly how long you have to reach positive cash flow and execute with confidence.

THE FOUNDER'S MATH HACK (MSP EXAMPLE)

The Founder's Math Hack cuts through financial noise to reveal the levers that truly drive impact. By simplifying complex reporting into a clear framework, it sharpens your decision-making and keeps your eyes on the big-picture trajectory.

	Proforma		
	Used to Vet Decisions		
VARIABLES	**MONTHLY**	**QUARTERLY**	**ANNUALLY**
Ordinary Income/Expense			
Income			
Agreement Overages	6,000	18,000	72,000
Hardware Income	85,000	255,000	1,020,000
Monthly Agreement Income 300,000	300,000	900,000	3,600,000
Project Income 75,000	75,000	225,000	900,000
Software Resale Revenue	20,000	60,000	240,000
Commission Revenue	4,000	12,000	48,000
Other Income	5,000	15,000	60,000
Total Income	**495,000**	**1,485,000**	**5,940,000**

		Proforma		
		Used to Vet Decisions		
	VARIABLES	**MONTHLY**	**QUARTERLY**	**ANNUALLY**
Cost of Goods Sold				
Technician Labor Costs	125,000	125,000	375,000	1,500,000
Hardware (COGS)		72,250	216,750	867,000
Software (COGS)		16,000	48,000	192,000
Managed Service (COGS)	75,000	75,000	225,000	900,000
Other COGS		10,000	30,000	120,000
5500 · Shipping		2,000	6,000	24,000
Total COGS		300,250	900,750	3,603,000
Gross Profit		**194,750**	**584,250**	**2,337,000**
Gross Profit Percent		**39%**		
Expense				
Management Labor	20,000	20,000	60,000	240,000
Sales & Marketing	30,000	30,000	90,000	360,000
Other Expense	58,000	58,000	174,000	696,000
Total Expense		**108,000**	**324,000**	**1,296,000**
Net Ordinary Income		**86,750**	**260,250**	**1,041,000**
Net Ordinary Income Percent	**17.53%**			
Cashflow Adjustments				
Debt Service				
Crap Debt Repayment		20,000	60,000	240,000
Total		**20,000**	**60,000**	**240,200**
Tax Escrow		34,700	104,100	416,400
Operating Cash Gain/Loss		**32,050**	**96,150**	**384,600**
Ratios				
MRR to Fixed Cost		**94.34%**		

DEBT MATRIX

Once liquidity targets are met, you are ready to "fix the balance sheet" by debt reduction. The north star of this exercise is to decrease cash flow pressure and increase free cash flow, so look at interest rate and payment terms.

1. Negotiate any vendors charging fees. This should be done as soon as possible, no reason to wait until liquidity targets are met. Remember: The goal is removing fees with consistent payments versus balance reduction. Balance reduction will force cash flow pressure.

2. Look for ways to reduce "crap debt." This is debt generated covering losses and has no redeeming qualities. It oftentimes consists of easy-to-access funds with high interest rates. Generally speaking, these are credit cards, factoring, maybe private loans.

3. Look for opportunities to free up cash flow. If you have debts with principal payments and low rates, try to renegotiate payments to free up more cash flow. If none, then start with the highest rates—unless another loan has principal payments that result in more cash flow to cover other debts, and the timeline to clear is reasonable.

4. Remember: Your lowest priority should be low-interest loans with reasonable repayment schedules.

Reminder: This becomes a math exercise and your north star is to free up cash flow to continue addressing debt to fix your balance sheet. Don't overthink it. Do some math, create a plan, and execute. Actually reducing debt is more important than making the best possible decision on which debt to pay.

Caution: Banks will not generally help you clean up "crap debt." Only once have I experienced a bank stepping in to refinance crap debt, and that was after nearly two years of solid operating cash flow—*and* it was an SBA loan because we were short on collateral. The SBA put a lien on the founders house (not just a guarantee) in order for the loan to be approved.

RUNWAY CALCULATOR

Establish a Timeframe

1. Start with your Go Forward Operating Plan and Founders Math Model for actions required to generate profitability and positive operating cash.

2. Estimate the length of time required to implement the actions required in your plan.

3. The next step is calculating positive operating cashflow. Based on step 2, add one cash cycle based on your average AR collection. Normally 30-45 days.

Real ex. from MSP recovery

Recovery plan and required actions	3 days
AR collection average	45 days
Timeline to calculate runway	48 days

Estimate Liquidity

4. Estimate cash requirements (ex. accrued payroll, vendor obligations prior to any negotiating, etc.) for the runway timeline established in steps 1-3.

    *   *Cash requirements in this step will be from periods prior to your actions to produce profitability*

5. Estimate cash receipts expected in the same period.

6. The next step is to calculate liquidity. Take current cash on hand plus estimated cash receipts in step 5 minus cash requirements in step 4.

Real ex. from MSP recovery

Cash on hand	
Estimated cash receipts	$ 360,000
Total	$ 360,000
Estimated cash requirements	$ (425,000)
Estimated liquidity	$ (65,000)

Estimate Deferred Obligations

7. Calculate deferred obligations such as AP in excess of terms, late loan payments, etc.

8. Estimate deferred obligations you will successfully negotiate .

9. Next step is to estimate deferred obligations to fund. Take deferred obligations in step 7 minus estimated negotiated obligations in step 8.

Real ex. from MSP recovery

Deferred obligations	$290,000
Estimate negotiated deferred obligations	$(275,000)
Estimated deferred obligations to fund	$15,000

Calculate Runway / Liquidity Gap

10. Take estimated liquidity from step 6 minus estimated deferred obligations from step 9.

11. Add a contingency of at least 25% (more is better).

Real ex. from MSP recovery

Estimated Liquidity	$ (65,000)
Estimated deferred obligations	$ (15,000)
	$ (80,000)
Contingency of 25% added	$ (100,000)

In this case, I knew we needed at least $100,000 or our recovery would likely fail. How did we fund it?

1. We borrowed from family members of the founder.

2. We were more successful in negotiating with creditors than estimated.

3. We received a large pre-paid order from a client which we set aside for liquidity.

Sometimes you're lucky or blessed! As a side note, we still give that client a huge discount fifteen years later as a quiet thank you for blessing us when they didn't even know it.

THE RUHLIN WAY—OUR PARTNERSHIP GUIDE

OPENING CONTEXT: A PARTNERSHIP GUIDE

What follows are philosophies I developed for John and me nearly eighteen years ago. I realized early on in our partnership that John and I see the world very differently. These philosophies helped align our thinking on how to manage our companies and opportunities. Perhaps you will find these thoughts helpful if you are in a partnership, or maybe they will be useful to align your team.

Disclosure: The Ruhlin Way are our guidelines, which doesn't necessarily mean they are the best fit for every partnership or organization.

1. **It's about the balance sheet.**

   The health of your organization is determined by the strength of your balance sheet. Large amounts of cash on hand provides flexibility, security, and opportunities during weak economic times. Don't be afraid to use appropriate amounts of leverage when necessary, but use as little as possible and tread softly. When you use debt, favor a longer repayment term over interest rate charged unless the rate is ridiculously high—in which case, you may not want to use it at all. Short repayment terms (even those with low rates) produce cash flow pressure, and we strive to avoid cash flow pressure at all costs. You can always pay off debt quicker than the term once the cash is produced, but you don't want to force your organization to produce high levels of cash flow to pay debt.

2. **Gross profit dollars produced drive earnings, not just revenue.**

   Too many organizations focus too much on sales and revenue rather than gross profit (i.e., sales per square foot and the like). Gross profit is what actually covers overhead and produces earnings. Sales, of course, is part of the equation, but not the only factor. Less revenue with higher margins is a more enjoyable way to live than high revenue with low margins.

3. **Distributable cash flow to shareholders/members is more important than earnings alone.**

   Earnings that require large amounts of ongoing capital investment mean shareholders/members will receive fewer distributions. Look for opportunities that require very little ongoing capital investment so you can maximize the dollars flowing to the shareholders/members.

4. **Build in a margin of safety into every deal that requires resources (capital or otherwise). Without one, walk away.**

   Enough said.

5. **Face brutal facts of reality and be "productively paranoid" about future prospects.[6]**

   Situations rarely improve on their own accord. Likewise, ignoring the brutal facts of reality doesn't mean they go away. Unfortunately, it *does* usually mean you are not prepared when "reality" happens. The best of the best organizations that have stood the test of time often have paranoid leaders.

---

6   Thanks again, Jim Collins!

Their paranoia drives them to be prepared to face the brutal facts of reality before they become crises. However, there is a warning: Make sure "productive paranoia" doesn't result in panic. Panic will never help. The positive outcome of healthy paranoia is focused urgency.

6. **Win with base hits and advancing runners versus just home runs. (In other words, don't live and die just on large deals. You want a solid and diverse customer base.)**

   Baseball teams that consistently get runners on base, advance runners, and manufacture runs can usually be competitive with more resourced teams and oftentimes beat them. Swinging for the fences can be exciting, but will often lead to solo shots and strike outs. In business, such volatility will cause stress and sleepless nights. Not to say that home runs are bad (they aren't!), but it's better to focus more of your organization's resources on producing those base hits. As a side benefit, a home run with runners on base means much more.

7. **Bet big only when the odds are clearly in your favor, you have done your empirical homework, and you have a margin of safety built in.**

   Shoot lots of bullets before cannons.

8. **Seek wise counsel or pay to get it when necessary.**

   Good advisers with the right experience are worth their weight in gold because they can save you the headaches, time, and stress caused by a poor decision. Plus, they become your cheerleaders.

9. **Only invest with partners you can trust.**
   A good deal with a so-so partner is not a good deal and will often result in regret. Rule of thumb: Assess the players involved in a deal first. Nothing else matters if you can't trust them.

10. **Don't die a hero. Concede the hill, conserve resources, and win the war.**
    Grit is critical for prolonged success, but you will lose some battles. Move on.

ABOUT THE AUTHOR

ROD NEUENSCHWANDER COFOUNDED GIFT·OLOGY WITH THE LATE John Ruhlin, author of *Gift·ology: The Art and Science of Using Gifts to Cut Through the Noise, Increase Referrals, and Strengthen Retention.* As the nation's leading relationship agency, Gift·ology helps clients accelerate growth by leveraging key relationships, with strategies featured in *Forbes, Business Insider,* and numerous podcasts.

Rod oversees operations and strategic objectives, continuing John's legacy of teaching that relationships achieve what marketing cannot. He also leads Ruhlin Partners, guiding struggling companies to recover, grow, and achieve over $30 million in founder wealth events.

An advocate for giving back, Rod has served as chair of Malone University's board of trustees and is deeply committed to supporting Christian organizations. He and his wife, Liz, along with their three children, enjoy quiet days by the pool and making generational impact through their time and resources.

TWO PATHS. ONE PHILOSOPHY.

Relationships move markets. Whether you're scaling word of mouth or staring down a make-or-break moment, your next move should build a legacy that lasts.

BUILD A RELATIONSHIP SYSTEM THAT SCALES

Want to build a business everyone talks about? If you believe:

- Relationships outperform ads
- Talent and culture drive customer satisfaction
- Word-of-mouth is your most underused asset

...it's time to systemize it.
Get started at *www.giftologygroup.com*

TURN CRISIS INTO LEGACY

If your business is in a make-or-break moment –perhaps facing one of the four crises outlined in the book—and you're ready to do something about it...

Rod Neuenschwander partners with a handful of high-stakes founders:

- From turnaround to wealth-creation events.
- Strategic direction, financial restraint, and emotional composure.
- Designed for founders with more to protect than just profit.
- "Rod brings a war room mindset to the boardroom moment."

Before you reach out, know this: We don't consult. We partner. We go all-in with strategy, sweat, and network. Or we don't go in at all.

If that's you, reach out: *www.businessonthebrink.com*
And let's build something worth remembering.

GIFT·OLOGY®

www.ingramcontent.com/pod-product-compliance
Lightning Source LLC
Chambersburg PA
CBHW021459180326
41458CB00051B/6878/J